PLAGUE-BUSTERS!

MEDICINE'S BATTLES WITH HISTORY'S
DEADLIEST DISEASES

T0035030

PLAGUE-BUSTERS!

MEDICINE'S BATTLES WITH HISTORY'S DEADLIEST DISEASES

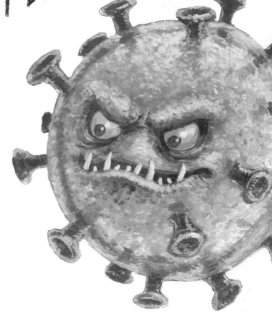

LINDSEY FITZHARRIS AND ADRIAN TEAL

ILLUSTRATED BY ADRIAN TEAL

BLOOMSBURY
CHILDREN'S BOOKS
NEW YORK   LONDON   OXFORD   NEW DELHI   SYDNEY

BLOOMSBURY CHILDREN'S BOOKS
Bloomsbury Publishing Inc., part of Bloomsbury Publishing Plc
1385 Broadway, New York, NY 10018

BLOOMSBURY, BLOOMSBURY CHILDREN'S BOOKS, and the Diana logo
are trademarks of Bloomsbury Publishing Plc

First published in the United States of America in October 2023
by Bloomsbury Children's Books

Text copyright © 2023 by Lindsey Fitzharris and Adrian Teal
Illustrations copyright © 2023 by Adrian Teal

All rights reserved. No part of this publication may be reproduced or transmitted in any form or by any means,
electronic or mechanical, including photocopying, recording, or any information storage or retrieval system, without
prior permission in writing from the publisher.

Bloomsbury books may be purchased for business or promotional use. For information on bulk purchases please
contact Macmillan Corporate and Premium Sales Department at specialmarkets@macmillan.com

Library of Congress Cataloging-in-Publication Data
Names: Fitzharris, Lindsey, author. | Teal, Adrian, author, illustrator.
Title: Plague-busters! : medicine's battles with history's deadliest diseases / by Lindsey Fitzharris and Adrian Teal ;
illustrated by Adrian Teal.
Description: New York : Bloomsbury Children's Books, 2023. | Includes bibliographical references and index.
Summary: This book delves into several illnesses that have infected humans and affected civilizations. Each chapter
explores the history of a specific disease, detailing the symptoms, cures, and medical breakthroughs that it spawned.
Identifiers: LCCN 2022059202 (print) | LCCN 2022059203 (e-book) |
ISBN 978-1-5476-0603-0 (hardcover) • ISBN 978-1-5476-0604-7 (e-book)
Subjects: LCSH: Plague—History—Juvenile literature. | Epidemics—History—Juvenile literature. |
Diseases and history—Juvenile literature.
Classification: LCC RC172 .F58 2023 (print) | LCC RC172 (e-book) | DDC 614.5/732—dc23/eng/20221223
LC record available at https://lccn.loc.gov/2022059202

Book design by John Candell
Printed and bound in India by Replika Press Pvt Ltd, Sonepat, Haryana
2 4 6 8 10 9 7 5 3 1

To find out more about our authors and books visit www.bloomsbury.com and sign up for our newsletters.

To our mothers, Debbie and Sandra.

· TABLE OF CONTENTS ·

PLAGUE-BUSTERS!

MEDICINE'S BATTLES WITH HISTORY'S
DEADLIEST DISEASES

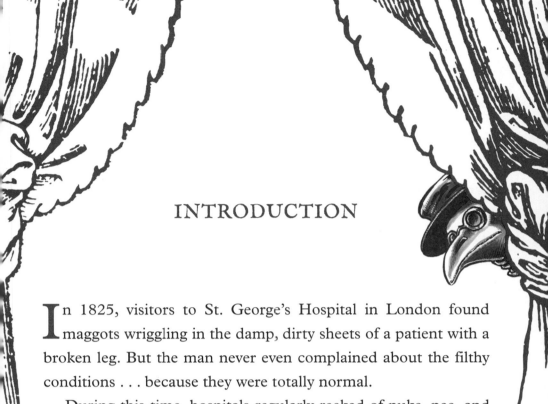

INTRODUCTION

In 1825, visitors to St. George's Hospital in London found maggots wriggling in the damp, dirty sheets of a patient with a broken leg. But the man never even complained about the filthy conditions . . . because they were totally normal.

During this time, hospitals regularly reeked of puke, pee, and poop. The smell was so horrible that the staff sometimes walked around with handkerchiefs pressed to their noses. Doctors didn't exactly smell like roses, either. They rarely cleaned their hands or their instruments and carried on them what they called "good old hospital stink." Hospitals were so infested with pesky lice that they had to employ bug-catchers, who were paid better than the surgeons! But they were fighting a losing battle.

Sounds weird, right? After all, cleanliness is crucial to keeping illnesses at bay . . . especially in a hospital! Well, we know this to be true today, of course. But the past can be a weird place. And the story of how medicine progresses isn't as straightforward as you might think.

Sometimes, doctors were wrong but clung to outdated ways of doing things, just because that was the way things had always been done. Other times, doctors were right, but no one listened to them. It's never been easy to convince people to change their habits.

For example, it may seem strange to us today, but washing your hands as a way to prevent sickness is a fairly recent measure. In the past, the idea that diseases could be spread by unclean hands didn't really cross many doctors' minds. But there was one man who saw things differently, tried to make a difference . . . and failed!

Ignaz Semmelweis was a Hungarian doctor in Vienna in the 1840s. There, he supervised two maternity wards, where expectant mothers went to give birth to their babies. One ward was run by male medical students, while the other was run by female midwives. Before long, Ignaz noticed something strange.

Although each ward was identical, the pregnant women looked after by the medical students were three times more likely to die than those who were looked after by the midwives. Ignaz wondered how this could be.

IGNAZ SEMMELWEIS

That was when he noticed that many medical students would leave the "dead house," where they cut up dead bodies to learn anatomy, and head straight onto the hospital wards. What if these medical students were carrying something nasty on their hands and were passing it on to the mothers when they delivered their babies?

Ignaz ordered all doctors to wash their hands before seeing their patients. Shortly afterward, the number of deaths decreased. His idea had worked!

But not everyone was happy with these changes. Many doctors resented having to wash their hands because they didn't understand why it was necessary. Even Ignaz couldn't explain it to them. He didn't know why his plan worked . . . he just knew that it did. But his colleagues thought it was just a fluke that pregnant women weren't dying any longer, and they made fun of poor Ignaz. They called him "the hand-washer," and he called them "murderers." Eventually, his colleagues got so fed up with Ignaz's accusations that they decided to take drastic action against him.

A doctor at the hospital tricked Ignaz into visiting what was called an "insane asylum," a prison-like place where people with mental disorders were treated, and often locked up permanently. You guessed it . . . they wanted to declare Ignaz insane so they could get rid of him. When Ignaz figured out what was happening, he tried to leave, but several guards blocked his way. They then beat him and locked him in a dark cell. A few weeks later, Ignaz died from his injuries.

It would be decades before doctors fully appreciated the value of handwashing.

So, like we said, the past proves that human progress has not been easy or straightforward. We're about to take you on a twisty-turny journey through the history of medicine. In this book, you'll discover a handful of epic tales about how some of the world's deadliest diseases were finally conquered thanks to a bunch of the biggest, most hard-won medical breakthroughs ever.

But all this isn't just about science and medicine. It's a story about people. It's a story about those who failed and those who succeeded, about those who benefited and those who were harmed. In these pages, you'll find genius and ignorance, kindness and cruelty, hard work and pure luck, and much more besides.

And we think that when we're done, you'll be convinced that right now is the best time to be alive!

PLAGUE,
OR
THE BLACK
DEATH

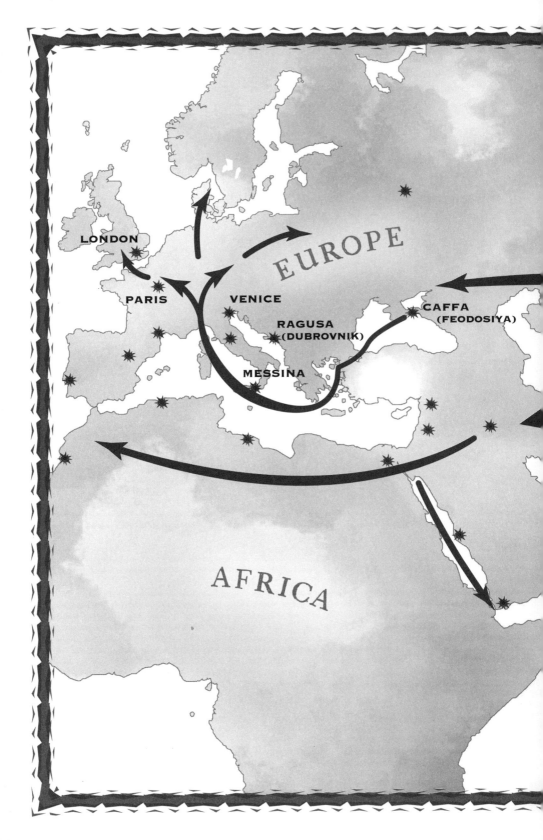

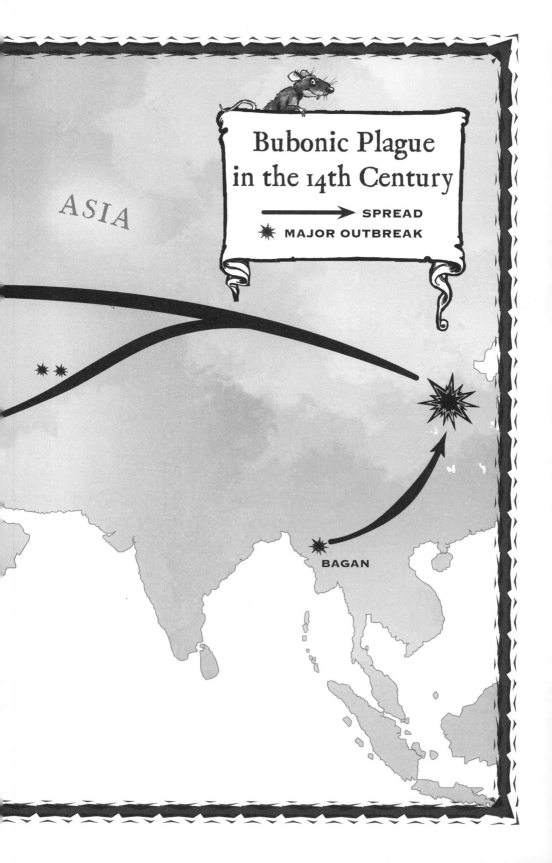

ASIA

Bubonic Plague in the 14th Century

→ SPREAD

✹ MAJOR OUTBREAK

BAGAN

CAFFA, ON THE BLACK SEA: 1346 CE

A huge and frightening army surrounds an important eastern trading port, sealing it off from the outside world. Nothing gets in, and nobody gets out.

The town of Caffa, on the northern coast of the Black Sea, has been holding out against this army of Mongols for some time. But now the soldiers are using a gross new tactic. Many of them have died from a strange sickness spreading through their ranks. So, their commander gives his weakened troops a terrible order. Using gigantic wooden catapults, the

army begins flinging the diseased bodies of dead soldiers over the city walls to terrify and kill Caffa's citizens.

Disease soon begins to spread within the town, but outside, the Mongol army continues to suffer too. Eventually, the sickly soldiers abandon the siege and march away.

With the army gone, Italian merchants who had been trapped in Caffa board their ships and sail west, toward their homelands. Some make for Genoa and Venice in the north of Italy. Some head farther south. In October 1347, a number of these merchant ships drop their anchors in the busy harbor of Messina.

Standing at the exact point where boot-shaped Italy gives the island of Sicily a gentle kick, Messina is a port that bustles with vessels and traders. News of sailors returning here from faraway lands is not at all unusual, but the people who gather to greet the ships are met with a horrible surprise. Most of the merchants aboard are dead, and the rest are barely clinging to life. They are feverish, sick, and mad with pain. Strangest of all, they are covered in ugly, black boils that ooze blood and pus. They have been struck down by the illness the Mongol soldiers had catapulted over Caffa's walls.

Almost at once, this unknown disease begins to attack the people who have tried to help the ships' crews. It spreads to more and more of Messina's terrified citizens. In the panic, many townsfolk flee to the countryside even as the ships are ordered out of the harbor. Soon, ports are closed elsewhere in Italy to try to stop the sickness from getting in. But it is too little, too late . . .

. . . THE BLACK DEATH HAS ARRIVED IN EUROPE!

Racing beyond Messina with terrifying speed, this disease will go on to kill around 25 million Europeans in the fourteenth century—or one in three people. Many believe the Black Death is a punishment from God and that asking for forgiveness for sin is their only hope of being saved. But some people turn to doctors for answers. Unfortunately, it will be a long fight before the mysteries of the Black Death are fully understood.

IF YOU'VE EVER DOUBTED that the past was a totally awful, hopeless, and disgusting place to live for a lot of the time, then we've got a stinking, sky-high pile of proof for you right here.

As far as medical disasters go, the Black Death (also called plague) was possibly the worst in human history and was certainly the grossest. It was named after the black swellings, or "buboes," that broke out on the necks, groins, or armpits of its victims. These buboes could grow as big as oranges. If the buboes burst on their own, there was some chance of survival. But usually they didn't burst, and people would die within hours or days of falling sick. Other effects of plague included stomach pain, violent puking, runny poops, fever, and chills. Your fingers, toes, and nose might also turn black as the tissue died, and you might experience bleeding under the skin or from the nose, mouth, or butthole. So, like we said . . . really not great.

Plague had been lurking around in the background for a long, long time. In 541 CE, it sprang up in Egypt. Two years later, it had hit countries around the eastern Mediterranean Sea and in the Middle East, killing a quarter of the population in the region. Because this happened during the reign of the Byzantine emperor Justinian, it became known as "Justinian's Plague" (which seems a bit unfair, as it really wasn't his fault). It reappeared from time

to time until the eighth century, including a major outbreak in England in 664 CE. Then it seemed to disappear.

But it would be back.

The first major outbreak happened between 1347 and 1351. During that time, tens of millions of people died. The Black Death raced along the trade routes between Asia and Europe, such as the one those unlucky Italian merchants used between Caffa and Messina. Then it rampaged through the filthy, overcrowded households and every town it could find.

Heading north through Europe, it arrived at a small port on the south coast of England in the summer of 1348. From there, it spread like . . . well, like the plague. The Scottish people in the north thought that God was punishing the English, who were their old enemies, and they decided to finish the job by invading England. But during their campaign, the Scottish army was hit by plague, and the sickness then swept through Scotland on their return home. It also arrived in Ireland via seaports at this time. And plague never seemed to go away. Between 1361 and 1362, there was a fresh outbreak that was especially hard on kids. This became known as the "mortality of children."

When plague broke out in London in 1563, Queen Elizabeth I moved her court to Windsor Castle outside the city. She had a set of gallows built there and ordered that anyone arriving from London was to be hanged in case they were carrying the disease.

Many Europeans thought plague was sent by God, who was angry with them about something or other, so gatherings and ceremonies were organized to apologize for sinning and to drive away

the evil demons. Unfortunately, bringing large groups of people together like this often helped spread the plague, not get rid of it. And even churchmen were not safe. In 1349, the Archbishop of Canterbury died of plague and was soon followed to the grave by his replacement.

God wasn't the only one who was blamed for spreading the plague. People accused lots of different groups, including the rich and people ill from a disease called leprosy. But they were all totally innocent. The rich were probably slightly less prone to infection simply because they didn't live in crowded conditions like everyone else. And though leprosy can cause skin sores, a bit like plague does, we now know the two diseases have absolutely nothing to do with each other.

While some played the blame game, there were other well-meaning people who tried to make sense of the plague using the best science around at the time. And that meant starting with something called the "four humors."

This is a really, really old idea about the human body that dates back to the ancient Greeks, who believed that the body was made up of four substances, or "humors": blood, phlegm, yellow bile, and black bile. When someone got sick, people thought that it meant the humors were out of whack. For example, a doctor might diagnose you as having too much blood in your body. So, they would deal with it by cutting one of your veins open and letting you bleed for a while.

This is all total nonsense, of course. But because the ancient Greeks were really smart and talented in lots of other fields—like politics, philosophy, and art—the idea stuck, and people believed in the four humors for centuries!

Those who weren't busy draining the blood out of plague victims were trying to figure out how the disease was spread, which was a more productive use of time. Some of the best guesses were that people got it by contagion (person-to-person contact) or by bad air, known as "miasma" [my-azz-ma]. In 1604, one way to test if the air in a room was "bad" was to shut a sheep in the room for a month, then wash the animal, give the water you used to your pigs, and see how they were affected. (Our guess is the pigs were probably just upset about having to drink someone else's bathwater, but whatever.)

Many remedies for plague were tried over the centuries, most of which proved to be hopeless—if not downright dangerous. These included the following:

- Wearing bags of arsenic against the skin or drinking mercury, both of which we now know to be deadly poisons. Interestingly, some people also wore bags of nutmeg around their necks, which may actually have been slightly effective. Nutmeg contains a natural insecticide that might have kept plague-carrying fleas at bay. But it was also fantastically expensive at the time, so it was probably not that practical.
- Eating crushed emeralds—if you were rich enough to afford them!
- Eating an exotic remedy called "Theriac" [theer-ee-ack], which originated in ancient Greece. It was also known as "treacle," and was originally a cure for snakebites. Later, it was thought to be an antidote for poisons. It had a whopping sixty-four ingredients, which included minerals, herbs, animal flesh, blood, and other substances that we now know are actually poisons—all mixed with honey.

I can see your nuggets!

💀 Rubbing herbs, onions, or slices of snake on the buboes, or cutting up a pigeon and rubbing it over the body. In the sixteenth century, the royal surgeon Thomas Vicary wrote about the benefits of plucking a live chicken's butt and holding it against a patient's buboes. We're guessing that didn't help.

💀 Burning herbs to purify the "bad" air in your house. Smoking tobacco was also believed to have curative powers. During the 1665 plague outbreak in London, the boys at Eton College were made to smoke pipes at breakfast! One kid who refused was whipped.

💀 Sitting next to a fire to drive out the fever or in a sewer where you were away from infected people (but very close to stinking streams of poop).

💀 Consulting doctors called "uroscopists" [yur-os-ko-pists]. These guys checked the color of patients' pee to figure out what was wrong with them. To do this, they used a chart called a "urine wheel," which showed how different-colored pee related to a person's state of health. Some docs even tasted the pee. The urine of people with diabetes can have a sweet flavor and smell, so this isn't quite as strange as it sounds—although it is as disgusting as it sounds!

 Bursting the buboes to drain the pus. A respected Italian doctor named Gentile da Foligno recommended doing this by pressing a hot plaster against the buboes, which forced them to split open. He missed the mark, though, when he said one of the plaster's ingredients should be dried human poop. Gentile also wrote a popular book on treating the Black Death, but then ruined his reputation by dying of plague himself.

Often, people suspected of carrying plague were not allowed to enter towns and cities. They were kept apart from everyone else to stop infection. The Republic of Ragusa (now part of modern-day Croatia) introduced this restriction in 1377 and locked up plaguey people for thirty days. In Venice in the 1400s, this period of isolation was given a name: "quarantine." It comes from the word for "forty," as people were typically held in that city for forty days. Although quarantine could be an effective way of protecting others, it must have made those suffering from plague feel lonely and scared.

Some people came super close to understanding the true cause of plague. In 1658, a clever German named Athanasius Kircher used a microscope to look at the blood of those who had died from the disease. He noticed what he called "little worms" in these samples. While he stopped short of describing these worms as "germs," his work did inspire a great deal of experimentation with the microscope. This would later lead to discoveries about the way disease is spread, and the microscope was to become a really essential gizmo in the world of medicine.

Plague kept coming and going for the next three hundred years. In different regions, rulers reacted to these outbreaks in different ways. For example, in Venice, there was one terrible episode in which tens of thousands of people were dying of plague. So, city leaders made a promise to God to build a cathedral if He would make the plague go away. It did go away, so in 1630, the leaders constructed the magnificent Basilica di Santa Maria della Salute, which still

sits at the mouth of the city's Grand Canal like a beautiful old grandma. But in Britain, where the last major outbreak

began in London in 1665, King Charles II and
his courtiers abandoned their capital city and
fled for Oxford some fifty miles away.

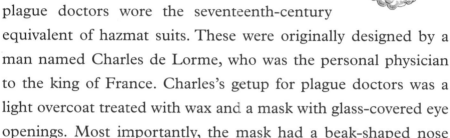

People with more backbone stuck around
and tried their best to help the sick. Dedicated
plague doctors wore the seventeenth-century
equivalent of hazmat suits. These were originally designed by a
man named Charles de Lorme, who was the personal physician
to the king of France. Charles's getup for plague doctors was a
light overcoat treated with wax and a mask with glass-covered eye
openings. Most importantly, the mask had a beak-shaped nose
with two "nostrils," and it was hollow inside.

The plague doctors stuffed the mask with a mixture of
strong-smelling things to keep at bay the "bad
air" that people thought was spreading
plague. This mixture could include
camphor (a plant extract), thyme, lemon
balm, garlic, and rose petals. (Another,
similar approach was to hold a posy
of sweet-smelling flowers to the
nose to ward off infectious air. To
this day, English judges continue
the custom by carrying small bunches of
flowers called "nosegays" on public occa-
sions!) The plague doctors also carried a
stick, and, from a safe distance, they used
it to point out what the patient's family
members should do to help them.

If plague struck a household, the building was sealed up to try to stop the sickness from moving door to door. These houses had red crosses painted on their doors, along with the words "Lord have mercy on us." At night, men would walk the streets with a cart and cry, "Bring out your dead!" Families would hand over the bodies of loved ones, which were put in the cart

and wheeled away to huge burial sites known as plague pits. Today, we know of around thirty-five plague pits in and around London.

Plague reappeared with a vengeance in the last half of the nineteenth century, causing a third pandemic (a fancy word for a worldwide outbreak, such as the one caused by COVID-19). During that time, around 15 million people died, with 10 million in India alone.

In 1894, a French scientist named Alexandre Yersin finally pinned down the cause of all this horror. He identified the plague germ in Hong Kong, while he was studying an outbreak in China. Meanwhile, a Japanese scientist called Shibasaburo Kitasato [Shee-ba-sa-bur-oh Kitta-sat-oh] was working on exactly the same outbreak, and he also found the germ—a kind known as a "bacterium"—at the same time as Alexandre. But it was Alexandre who got the credit, and history's most terrifying

ALEXANDRE YERSIN

and disgusting disease is now called *Yersinia pestis* [yur-sinny-ah pest-iss] after him. His mother would have been very proud. The following year, Alexandre set up a laboratory where he prepared treatments against the plague.

George Rae was appointed Edinburgh's "plague doctor" in 1645 after the first one died. He was promised a large fee as it was expected that he too would die before he could collect the money. Rae tended to the sick and survived. He spent the next decade trying to collect the fee—with no success.

In recent years, scientists have tested the skeletons of some ancient plague victims and have confirmed that *Yersinia pestis* was indeed to blame. We now know much more about how plague spreads too. It mostly finds its way into humans thanks to fleas living on animals, such as rats. Rats made their homes alongside people in the nooks and crannies of over-crowded cities. They also stowed away on ships, helping to spread the disease far and wide.

When there were outbreaks of plague, many rats would die, and their fleas had to look elsewhere for blood to suck. So, they picked on people! The plague bacteria blocked the path to the flea's stomach, so when the flea next tried to suck blood, the blockage made it puke the bacteria into the bloodstream of the animal or person it was biting.

There are different forms of plague, and before modern treatments, they had different levels of deadliness. Bubonic plague—named after those revolting buboes—would kill half of those who caught it. Meanwhile, nine out of ten of those with the kind called pneumonic [new-mon-ick] plague usually died within one or two days, actually drowning on dry land from the fluid that filled their lungs. This form of plague had you coughing droplets containing the bacteria into the air. These droplets might be breathed in by someone close by, causing that person to fall sick too. Airborne droplets are the only way that plague can spread from one person to another. The third and final form, septicemic [sept-a-seem-ick] plague, infected the blood, rapidly killing every single one of its victims.

Plague is still around. But thanks to medical science, it can be cured today with several kinds of antibiotics—the first of which was found pretty much by accident.

In the 1660s, a man named Samuel Pepys [Peeps] kept a diary of his everyday life in London. When the plague struck in 1665, he wrote about how some people blamed the spread of the disease on wigs that might have been made from the hair of plague victims. Samuel himself bought into the rumor and noted in his diary that he didn't dare wear a fancy new wig he had bought in case he got sick.

In 1928, a Scottish scientist named Alexander Fleming was researching germs. One day he noticed a blob of mold in one of his petri dishes, which was supposed to be growing bacteria. No bacteria were growing around the mold, so the mold was clearly killing them off. Alexander called the mold's active ingredient "penicillin."

ALEXANDER FLEMING

After a lot of hard work, penicillin became one of the world's most widely used medications for fighting bacteria. It has led to a whole host of other useful antibiotics and has saved countless lives. It's a good thing that Alexander was both lucky and clever—we have him to thank for unleashing the life-changing powers of icky green mold!

Famous Deaths from Plague

1348: Joan Plantagenet,
Daughter of King Edward III of England

Joan was only fourteen when she was sent to marry a Spanish prince, who was later known as Pedro the Cruel. Joan journeyed in style, with hundreds of people and armed men in attendance, and with a beautifully decorated traveling chapel so that she could go to church services. But while on her journey, she stopped in the French city of Bordeaux, where plague was raging. Joan and her party stuck around too long, and she fell ill. In a small village called Loremo, she became one of the plague's first royal deaths.

1534: The Family of Nostradamus, Plague Doctor and Astrologer

Nostradamus was a seer, which is someone who predicts the future (or claims to). Many people who have studied his work think he predicted events like the rise of Adolf Hitler and the Great Fire of London. But his writings are so vague and mysterious that they allow people to see in them what they want to see. However, when he wasn't "seeing" into the future, Nostradamus was also a doctor who became famous for saving many plague victims in France and Italy. Unlike other doctors, who used harmful "cures," Nostradamus used hygiene and other sensible methods, like the removal of dead bodies from the streets. He created a pill for plague made from rose hips, which we now know contain high levels of health-giving vitamin C. But sadly, he couldn't save his own family—his wife and two kids died of plague.

1558: Joan, Elder Sister of the Playwright William Shakespeare

Joan was the first child William Shakespeare's parents had, but she died of plague shortly after her birth. Later, her parents had another child whom they also named Joan, who lived well into

her seventies. In the year of William's birth (1564), another outbreak of plague killed around a quarter of the population of his hometown, Stratford-upon-Avon, and it often sprang up there in the summertime. The disease had a big impact on William's life, and he mentions the plague in many of his plays. The theaters in London at the time were usually the first public spaces to be closed when plague was raging, and William's wallet would have taken a big hit when this happened.

1576: Titian, the Artist

Titian's full name was Tiziano Vecellio. He was one of the greatest painters of sixteenth-century Venice. His last painting was his *Pietà*—an image of the Virgin Mary holding her dead son, Jesus—and he worked on it while Venice was being ravaged by plague. He painted it to be hung at his grave site, and at the bottom of the scene he included a plaque on which he and his son Orazio are shown praying to be saved from plague. Sadly, this prayer was unanswered, and both he and Orazio died. The unfinished painting had to be completed by one of his students. Titian was the only victim of the Venice plague to be given a church burial. Despite this honor, his mansion was looted by thieves.

LONDON: AUGUST 1721

L ice as big as pine needles crunch under the soles of surgeon Charles
Maitland's boots as he winds his way through Britain's most infamous prison: Newgate.

All around him, the wails and screeches of prisoners ring out. The jail is disgustingly dank during these humid summer months. Charles clutches at the wet stone walls, feeling his way through the darkness. There are few windows, and the surgeon must strain to see in the gloomy passageways.

Strapped under Charles's nose is a small bundle of sweet-smelling herbs to mask the terrible stink of five hundred bodies living, breathing, and pooping alongside the animals that are kept in the prison to feed its growing population.

Since its founding in the Middle Ages, Newgate Prison has become a symbol of death and suffering. Prisoners are clapped in heavy irons when they arrive and held in tiny cells, each one housing half a dozen inmates or more. The prison itself is filthy. Only a quarter of those awaiting execution

make it to their own hanging. The rest die from starvation or disease. Those who do survive have to listen to a haunting midnight tradition on the night before executions. A local church minister walks slowly through the corridors, ringing a bell and chanting, "All you that in the condemned hold do lie, prepare you, for tomorrow you shall die."

A few days before Charles Maitland steps inside the prison, six convicts had been moved to a separate holding cell. The scruffy group, consisting of three men and three women, are guilty of nothing more serious than petty theft. But at a time when most crimes are punishable by death, stealing a silk handkerchief or a powdered wig often wins the thief an appointment with the hangman. Days before their executions, however, these frightened prisoners are being given a rare chance to escape the noose and walk out of Newgate free.

There is just one catch.

Charles pauses outside the prisoners' cell as the jailer fumbles with a heavy set of keys. Once unlocked, the door creaks open, and the surgeon steps over the threshold. Crammed inside the damp, stuffy chamber alongside the prisoners are dozens of important doctors from a major scientific institute called the Royal Society. They have been invited there as witnesses. The room is buzzing with excitement. In Charles's hand is a small glass container of infectious pus that has been scraped from the sores of someone who, just a few hours earlier, died from smallpox—one of the most dreaded diseases in history.

Some of the prisoners, already terrified, begin to tremble at the sight of the surgeon. An experiment is about to begin.

SMALLPOX SOUNDS SIMILAR TO a childhood disease called chicken pox. Today, chicken pox isn't very common in the United

States, but your teacher or parents might have caught it when they were younger. Both smallpox and chicken pox cause rashes and blisters. They each have "pox" in their names. But you should think of smallpox as chicken pox's evil twin. Chicken pox is the brother who's a minor pain in the butt. He'll give you a noogie and run off with your Halloween candy. Smallpox is the wicked brother with bloodshot eyes, a chainsaw, and a gigantic attitude problem. He killed more than three hundred million people in the twentieth century alone!

The name "smallpox" comes from the pus-filled blisters, or pocks, that form all over a victim's body. In many cases, the pocks turn black, giving the skin a charred look. In really bad cases, patients can be blinded if the rash breaks out too close to the eyes, or they can be left with deep scars called "pockmarks," assuming they don't die first.

We now know that smallpox is caused by a tiny germ called the "variola" [vair-ee-oh-luh] virus. Nobody knows for sure where variola came from, but it might have first appeared in Egypt at least three thousand years ago. Scientists have found evidence of the virus in the rashes that scar the faces of ancient mummies. Later, in the second century CE, the Roman Empire was hit by a terrible wave of sickness that might have been smallpox. As the centuries passed, the disease appeared to be unstoppable, spreading around the globe.

Spanish and Portuguese conquistadors brought smallpox into the New World after the explorer Christopher Columbus led the way there in 1492. The Aztec and Inca peoples had never been exposed to the disease, so they didn't have the natural resistance to it that had built up over time in other populations. The consequences were disastrous and led to the fall of their civilizations. For the same reason, indigenous peoples in North America also died in great numbers after coming into contact with European colonizers. Sadly, entire tribes were wiped out by smallpox.

By the eighteenth century, four hundred thousand people were dying of smallpox *each year* in Europe. The virus, which some people called "the speckled monster" due to its disfiguring effects, had become a common and terrifying threat to all humanity.

There was no cure for smallpox, and there still isn't. Prevention has always been the best hope, and we'll talk more about that shortly. But a few people did try to come up with ways to treat it.

In the 1300s, a man named John of Gaddesden was convinced that the color red could cure smallpox. Because he was the doctor to the king of England, people listened to him. He thought that patients should be covered in red cloth, surrounded by red decorations, and fed only red foods. This became a popular treatment for such a long time that two hundred years later, Queen Elizabeth I was wrapped in red cloth after she fell ill with smallpox. Some hospital wards even had red lamps, red curtains, and red walls.

It all sounds ridiculous, but might there have been something to it? In 1893, a Danish scientist named Niels Ryberg Finsen found that exposing people with smallpox to red light didn't cure them, but it did prevent their sores from weeping pus and leaving pockmarks. We now know that if the red light used is strong enough, it can pass through the skin into the layers below. Then, as it's absorbed by our cells, it can trigger the production of collagen, which is the stuff that holds our bodies together. Collagen helps us heal, improves our circulation, and increases the amount of oxygen going to our cells. Red light also lessens inflammation and fights bacteria. So, maybe John of Gaddesden was on to something after all!

Some treatments for smallpox were harsher. In the seventeenth century, another English doctor named Thomas Sydenham tortured a patient while trying to cure him. After taking a pint of his blood, Thomas ordered the man to lie in bed with the sheets no higher than his waist. Thomas kept the patient cold by leaving the windows open for days in a row. Each day, he also made the man drink twelve bottles of beer that were laced with sulfuric acid—which, in large doses, can burn holes in the stomach. Amazingly, the man survived. But trust us . . . it was no thanks to his doctor.

When it came to *preventing* smallpox, though, there was hope on the horizon.

The medical experiment at Newgate Prison in 1721 was the brain-child of an Englishwoman named Lady Mary Wortley Montagu, who was the daughter of a duke.

Lady Mary was no stranger to smallpox. In 1713, her brother caught the virus and died, leaving behind two children and a wife. Two years later, she caught the virus herself. Although she did recover, her face was scarred for life with pockmarks.

A short while later, Lady Mary and her family moved to the city of Constantinople (now Istanbul, in Turkey) because her husband had been made an ambassador. There, she learned of a very old practice. It involved inserting pus from a sick person into a cut in the skin of a healthy person. (Sometimes it was performed by having people sniff the dust from the scabs on drying smallpox sores!) This would cause the healthy person to develop a mild case of smallpox. But why would this be a good thing?

Variolation—as it was often called—had also been practiced in East Asia for hundreds of years. In the late seventeenth century, traders carrying goods from

Onesimus was an enslaved man in Boston in the early eighteenth century. He told his enslaver, a preacher named Cotton Mather, about how he had been variolated against smallpox as a child in Africa. As a result, Cotton campaigned for variolation during a smallpox outbreak in the city in 1721. But because the idea came from a Black man, the pigheaded townsfolk were totally against the idea, and only a few agreed to undergo the procedure. As a result, 844 Bostonians died . . . many of them unnecessarily.

Persia and China had imported the technique to Constantinople. If done correctly, variolation could protect you from getting smallpox by giving you "immunity." If you are immune to a disease, it means your body knows how to fight it off. This often happens after you get sick from a bug. Ideally, variolation would provide immunity, without making you quite as sick as smallpox would. But variolation carried its own risks.

The main danger lay in the amount of virus lurking in the pus taken from the infected person: too little had no effect, while too much could kill you. Complicating matters was the fact that anyone who was variolated became contagious for a short period and could spread the virus to others. Because of this, patients had to be kept apart from everyone for weeks. So, as well as being risky, it was time-consuming and came at a cost, since a variolated person couldn't work while recovering from the procedure.

With the horrors of smallpox still fresh in her mind, Lady Mary was convinced that the benefits of variolation outweighed the difficulties. She asked her doctor, Charles Maitland—who had accompanied her family to Constantinople—to perform the procedure on her son. He did so with great success.

On Lady Mary's return to Britain, she began singing the praises of variolation. Unfortunately, she quickly discovered that many doctors were unwilling to risk their reputation on an untested treatment. So, in June 1721, Charles Maitland, along with several other medical men, asked King George I for permission to carry out an experiment—one that no doctor would be allowed to do today! They wanted to variolate six prisoners from Newgate

Prison. If the men and women survived, they would be granted an official pardon and set free. The king, who was eager to ensure variolation was safe so that his own grandchildren could be protected against smallpox, boldly agreed to let someone else take all the risk.

Several court physicians and members of the Royal Society crowded into Newgate Prison to watch the experiment. As it turned out, all the prisoners survived, and those who were exposed to smallpox later proved to be immune to the virus. The experiment had worked!

But concerns about the safety of the procedure lingered. And so, a few months later, Charles Maitland repeated the experiment—this time on orphaned children (something that would also be prohibited today). Fortunately for him and the orphans, it was a triumph. Finally, on April 17, 1722, the king granted Charles permission to variolate the royal grandchildren. Unsurprisingly, variolation won a lot of support after this last success.

Although it had its risks, variolation was the best form of defense against smallpox for a while. That was until an English doctor named Edward Jenner discovered vaccination at the end of the eighteenth century.

Edward was born in 1749 and became an apprentice to a country surgeon when he was only thirteen years old so that he could learn the trade. His journey to his great discovery began when he heard a milkmaid boast that she would never catch smallpox because she had already suffered from cowpox. This was a virus mainly found in cows, but humans sometimes caught it while milking the animals' infected udders. Cowpox caused symptoms resembling mild smallpox. The milkmaid's claim stuck in Edward's mind, and he began to wonder whether he could use this information to swing the battle against smallpox in medicine's favor.

Edward put his thinking to the test many years later when Sarah Nelmes, the daughter of a local farmer, came to him seeking relief from sores that had recently appeared all over her body. Sarah was certain she knew the culprit: her beloved brown-and-white cow, Blossom.

Edward remembered what the milkmaid had said long ago and decided to try an experiment to see if cowpox really could protect someone from catching the deadlier smallpox. He made a small cut in a pustule on Sarah's hand and collected the pale liquid that seeped from it. In

In 1805, the French military leader Napoleon Bonaparte made vaccination compulsory for his armies. He also awarded a medal to Edward Jenner in spite of the fact that France was at war with Britain. At Edward's request, Napoleon released two English prisoners of war and allowed them to return home. The French general reportedly said that he could not "refuse anything to one of the greatest benefactors of mankind."

May 1796, he used this pus to infect his very first patient: James Phipps, an eight-year-old local boy, whose name was about to become famous in the science and history of vaccination.

Following the procedure, James experienced a headache, chills, and loss of appetite. Six weeks later, Edward attempted to variolate James with the smallpox virus. Normally, this would have given him a mild case of smallpox. But miraculously, James developed no symptoms. The cowpox had protected him against the smallpox. Edward had totally nailed it with his experiment.

Edward invented the word "vaccination" to describe this new technique—a safer alternative to variolation with similar benefits. It comes from the Latin word *vaccinus*, which means "of or from the cow." This made sense to Edward since his vaccine was made from cowpox. And although the vast majority of vaccines today have no connection to cows whatsoever, the name has stuck.

The vaccine was such a success that one of Edward's friends

told him that if he kept its ingredients a secret, he might make as much as £100,000 from it. That's a lot of money, even today! But Edward wasn't interested in getting rich from his discovery. He just wanted to save lives. And so, he published his research, and then began vaccinating everyone who came to visit him at his home in the countryside. He even built a hut in his garden to treat patients, which he called the "Temple of Vaccinia." Not only was

the temple a beacon of hope for the poor who needed protection against smallpox, but the work Edward did there also made it the site of the first public health service in Britain.

News of Edward's vaccine spread as fast as a horse could gallop, and it wasn't long before the country doctor was famous. Though he never left England, Edward became celebrated the world over. Thomas Jefferson, the third president of the United States, told

Not everybody sang Edward's praises. As news of his vaccine spread, a rash of sensationalist stories broke out, with false rumors about possible side effects. There was poor Sarah Burley, "whose face was distorted, and began to resemble that of an Ox." And little Edward Gee, "who was covered with sores, and afterwards with patches of Cow's Hair." Four-month-old William Ince reportedly "grew horns as a result of being cowpoxed." It seemed that suddenly children all over the world were developing cowlike features as a result of being vaccinated with cowpox! The only snag for Edward's enemies was that none of these stories was true.

Edward in a letter that "mankind can never forget that you have lived."

But Edward knew he wasn't the only one who should be honored. When Sarah's cow, Blossom, eventually died, Edward displayed her horns, hide, and tail in his home to remind people of her contribution to his discovery.

Edward's lifelong dream to rid the world of smallpox was fulfilled in May 1980 when the World Health Organization (WHO)

announced that the virus had at long last been conquered. The victory, which saved countless lives, was partly thanks to a campaign of vaccination, led by an American doctor and "disease detective" named Donald A. Henderson. It was an extraordinary moment in the history of medicine, and now the only smallpox samples left in the world exist under lock and key in medical laboratories. Because of this triumph, nobody can catch or die from smallpox today!

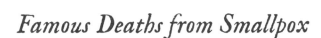

Famous Deaths from Smallpox

1145 BCE: Ramses V, Pharaoh of Ancient Egypt

Ramses ruled Egypt for only about four years before dying suddenly in his thirties. Some of the world's earliest evidence of smallpox has been found in his mummified body, and his dried-up skin still shows signs of the disease's tell-tale pustules. The deaths of Ramses and other family members were unexpected, and they weren't buried right away. Were these delays due to precautions over handling diseased bodies during a smallpox epidemic?

I feel terrible

1694: Queen Mary II of England

One morning in 1694, Queen Mary II awoke to find her arms covered in pustules. Thinking she had smallpox, she began to plan for her death. But after Mary was treated by her doctors, she seemed to get better. Did she have a simple case of measles, a less deadly disease with similar symptoms? Well, no. It was actually the really bad form of smallpox that causes bleeding inside the body and under the skin, eventually giving patients a blackened or charred look. Mary's "recovery" was short-lived: she died one night next to her husband, King William, who was sleeping in a small bed at her side.

1736: Francis Folger Franklin, Son of Benjamin Franklin

In 1736, Benjamin Franklin, who later helped draft the Declaration of Independence, lost his four-year-old son, Francis, to

smallpox. In later life, he wrote about his deep regret at not having had the young boy variolated. In fact, Benjamin had planned to do so, but Francis had been ill at the time, and the procedure was never rescheduled. Benjamin urged other parents not to make the same mistake.

1861: Henry Gray, Anatomist

Henry Gray was a brilliant young surgeon who made his name with a study of the nerves of the human eye. He became a very important and respected teacher of anatomy in Britain and published an incredibly famous book on the subject, which is still used by medical students today. It's known as *Gray's Anatomy*. In 1861, Henry nursed his nephew, Charles, back to health after the boy had caught smallpox. In the process, however, Henry caught the disease himself and died at the young age of thirty-four. All his possessions, including his unpublished writings, were burned as a precaution.

1870: Jules Léotard, French Acrobat

Jules dodged a career as a lawyer to become a famous trapeze artist. He was the first acrobat to jump from one trapeze to another and to perform a midair somersault. His stunts inspired the song "The Daring Young Man on the Flying Trapeze." In 1861, Jules was paid a small fortune to perform his trapeze act in London, above the heads of people having dinner. To show off his muscles, he invented the skintight piece of clothing that now bears his name: the leotard. But in Spain, Jules's life was cut short by smallpox, or maybe cholera (a disease we'll frighten you with later).

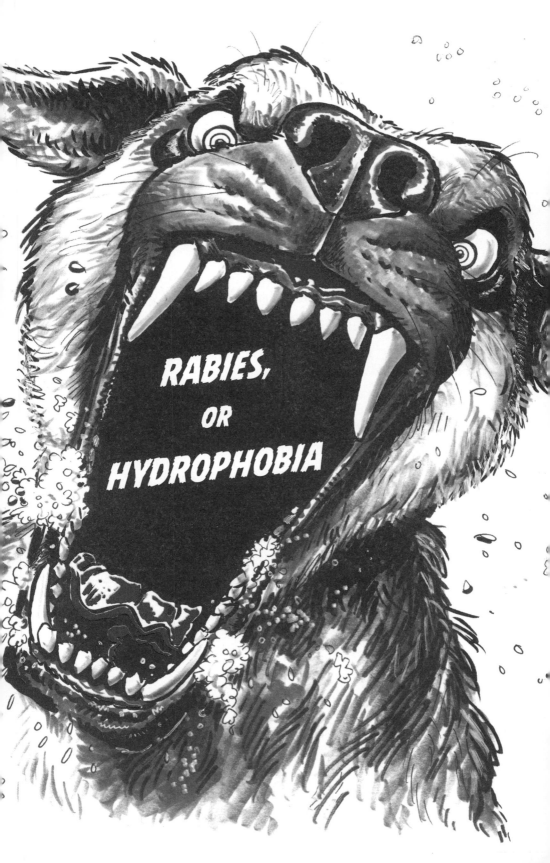

LONDON: THE SUMMER OF 1760

There is panic on the streets. Danger is lurking around every corner, and nobody feels safe. Rumors and scare stories fuel the fear, and the press isn't helping matters. For weeks, the newspapers have been full of terrifying reports about savage attacks on innocent citizens of old London town. And the suspect is a peculiar one: stray dogs!

Ye Olde Police Dept.

K9-NUT5

The dogs are infected with rabies—a truly horrible disease that almost always ends in death. The dogs catch rabies through the bites of other infected animals and then pass it to humans by biting them too. After someone has been infected, the site of the bite might start to itch. In fact, it can get so itchy that the person might even tear their skin as they scratch at the wound! Later, they may develop a fever or headache, and they might begin to feel anxious and generally unwell. They may also experience confusion or violent behavior, hallucinations, muscle spasms, and difficulty breathing.

In parts of the southwestern United States, rabies was commonly found in spotted skunks in the nineteenth century. Because of this, settlers often called these animals "hydrophobia cats," or "phobey cats" for short. Unfortunately, the spotted skunk's reputation as a carrier of rabies led to its being overhunted. As a result, it's hard to spot a spotted skunk in certain states today!

Rabies is also known as "hydrophobia," which means "fear of water," because the affected person often has trouble drinking due to unbearable throat pain. In extreme cases, just seeing water can cause panic in someone infected with rabies. They often can't even swallow their own spit, which causes them to drool.

News of people contracting rabies in London comes in thick and fast during the summer of 1760. The London Chronicle alone publishes dozens of reports. One story describes a child whose hand had been bitten by a rabid dog: the story goes that her parents had her arm cut off to prevent the infection from spreading. Another article reports that a tradesman who had been attacked by a stray dog was so fearful of contracting rabies that he later died of fright. There is even a rumor that a nine-year-old girl began barking after she had been bitten by a "mad dog." The newspapers are full of such weird tales! The fear gripping the city grows and grows.

With public alarm at fever pitch, the city leaders decide it's time for an extreme solution. They issue an order that any Londoner willing to kill a stray dog over the next two months will be paid a reward. Eager to make money, many people take to the streets with clubs looking for dogs on the loose. But not everyone agrees with the order. Many animal lovers feel these measures are terrible and cruel.

Even England's most famous artist is dragged into the argument. His name is William Hogarth, and he is known for brilliant paintings and prints that make fun of the people and the world around him. He is also

WILLIAM HOGARTH

the proud owner of a pet pug, which he sometimes paints into his own pictures. But William becomes the butt of jokes himself after a fellow artist publishes a drawing of him crying about the danger to his pug, as he watches men chase dogs through the streets.

How long will this panic last?

DON'T WORRY . . . NOBODY ACTUALLY killed William Hogarth's beloved pug. But the rabies outbreak was real enough and lasted for three years. Eventually, after many of the infected dogs were rounded up and others just died off, calm returned to London.

Rabies had been striking fear into people's hearts long before the summer of 1760, though. Humans and dogs first became friends somewhere between fourteen thousand and thirty-two thousand years ago, and this was great for the dogs and for us. But where there were pooches, there could also, sometimes, be rabies.

The first written record of rabies killing dogs and people is found in the Mesopotamian Laws of Eshnunna—a bunch of

rules written on clay tablets from around 1930 BCE in what is now the country of Iraq. One law stated that people had to pay a fine if their "mad" dog caused someone's death. In fact, for thousands of years, humans have known that a bite from an infected animal could lead to a bad death. And because an injured person didn't always get sick straightaway after being bitten, they might sit around fretting for weeks, not knowing whether they were going to die from rabies or not.

In the past, many people believed that dogs were more likely to get rabies when there had been an eclipse of the moon—but they were super wrong. Even so, some folks seemed to understand that rabies was caused by something in the spit, or saliva, of the sick animal. They just didn't know what that something was. In the fourth century BCE, a clever ancient Greek guy named Aristotle noted that rabies killed both the infected dog and any animal it had bitten. But the disease wouldn't be properly understood or treated for many centuries.

Nearly all cases of rabies in humans are caused by dogs. But it has been passed on to people from other animals too.

For example, around 900 CE, a rabid bear charged into the French city of Lyon. It attacked twenty people, six of whom fell sick with the "madness." To put them out of their

misery, the townspeople suffocated them in their sleep. And in 1271, thirty people died in the north of Germany after being bitten by a pack of rabid wolves. In France, many people, dogs, and pigs were bitten by rabid foxes, and on one occasion, a lone wolf with rabies bit forty-six people and eighty-two cows in one day.

By the nineteenth century, rabies had become a big problem in Europe. With no successful ways to treat it, measures were taken to control its spread. For instance, in Britain, a law was passed that let the police round up all stray dogs. As a result, rabies became much less common. By the early twentieth century, there was almost no rabies in the country at all. A few cases still popped up, though. At the end of the First World War, rabies returned to Britain when soldiers brought home infected dogs. Thankfully, the outbreak was quickly contained.

For a very long time, the only way to deal with rabies was to avoid getting it. People were so scared of the disease that some patients even took their own lives if they thought they had become infected. Although there were those who did try to find a cure, many of their ideas were as wild as the rabid dogs themselves.

For example, an ancient Roman doctor named Celsus suggested the sickness was carried in a dog's saliva, which was true. However, he also thought that rabies patients should be thrown

into a lake or river to cure them of their fear of drinking. Those who couldn't swim would swallow water as they sank. Those who could swim should be held under the surface until they too swallowed water. In Celsus's mind, this would solve the problem. To be fair, drowning people was certainly one way to stop them from feeling sick!

Other "cures" were just as bonkers, such as eating the liver of the sick animal or burning the bite wound with a hot iron. In the Middle Ages, a friar named Albert the Great believed that you could cure a dog with rabies by hanging it by its paws in a bath for over a week, shaving it bare and rubbing beet juice all over it, then hanging it in the bath again.

Those who didn't want to own a savage, naked, bright pink dog often turned to religion for answers. A story went around

that Bishop Hubert of Liège in Belgium had been visited by Saint Peter, who gave him a golden key with amazing powers. Hubert later used the magical key to cure a man bitten by a rabid dog—or so he claimed.

After Hubert's death, he was made a saint, and pilgrims would visit his church for blessings that they believed would protect them from rabies. The church sold copies of the key, which the pilgrims would hang in their homes for protection. Sometimes they would heat up the keys and use them to brand dogs to stop them from getting the disease. They would also use them to burn the wounds of bite victims to encourage healing. Saint Hubert's keys were used throughout Europe to ward off rabies for more than a thousand years.

In America, "madstones" took the country by storm as a possible cure for rabies in the nineteenth century. These stones were

According to legend, werewolves are people who morph into vicious, bloodthirsty wolves or are a mutant combination of human and wolf. Their mythical lust for killing people and animals may have been inspired by rabies patients, who show similar violent tendencies when suffering from the virus.

actually hardened hairballs found in the stomachs of animals such as goats and cows. The ones found inside deer were the most prized madstones of all and were believed to have amazing healing powers. Treatment began by boiling the madstone in sweetened milk or water to purify it. It was then pressed to the wound to draw the "poison" out. Madstones were used not just to treat rabies, but also bites from snakes and spiders. In fact, so treasured were these

objects that they were often passed down through families as precious heirlooms. Madstones were even more valuable than some gemstones. In 1805, one was sold in Virginia for $2,000—which would be about $44,000 in today's money!

Happily, the days of relying on madstones and magic keys to "cure" rabies were numbered, thanks to a clever French scientist named Louis Pasteur [Loo-ee Past-ur]. Nearly ninety years after the English doctor Edward Jenner created the first human vaccine against smallpox, Louis would make the first human vaccine against rabies. And, just like Edward, his first patient would be a young boy.

Louis got famous long before he turned his mind to curing rabies. In the 1860s, he showed that bacteria were to blame for souring wine, beer, and even milk. To stop this from happening,

LOUIS PASTEUR

Louis invented a simple procedure that involved heating these liquids to a high temperature to kill the microorganisms—a process now known as "pasteurization." His work would eventually give rise to the theory that many diseases are also caused by bacteria and other microorganisms, or "germs."

In the 1870s, Louis started studying chicken cholera, a disease

that was killing France's poultry. He figured that if a vaccine could be found for smallpox, vaccines could be found for all diseases—even those affecting animals. He began by isolating the bacterium that caused chicken cholera and then injecting small amounts of it into healthy chickens to build up their resistance. Unfortunately, many of the birds died.

Then something great happened by a total fluke, which is often how scientific discoveries are made!

One day, Louis asked his assistant to repeat the original experiment and inject a new batch of chickens with the bacterium. The assistant, however, was about to go on vacation and forgot to complete the task. On his return, he injected the chickens. At this point, the bacteria were weeks old. As a result, the chickens only developed a mild form of the disease. None of them died—but had they built up any immunity? After a while, Louis injected the same chickens with fresh bacteria. This time, the chickens did not get sick: they had built up resistance to the disease thanks to the weakened, old bacteria. Louis (thanks to his featherbrained assistant) had solved the mystery of how to create a vaccine that would protect the chickens, not kill them.

In the early 1880s, Louis turned his attention to rabies. Although dogs were the most common carriers of the disease, Louis decided to use rabbits for his experiments because it was easier to deal with a bunch of small bunnies than a laboratory full of rowdy mutts. However, unlike cholera, which is caused by bacteria, he had no idea that rabies is caused by a virus—a germ that was too small to see with the microscopes of the time. And viruses "mutate," or change quickly, as we've seen with COVID-19. This makes them more difficult to work with than bacteria. By infecting rabbits with rabies, Louis accidentally forced the virus to adapt to a new species, which could have created big problems. But luckily for Louis, after this virus mutated in the rabbits, it became less

dangerous to other animals. It was another fantastic lucky break for science! The vaccine that Louis created with help from his rabid rabbits wasn't just effective, but also safer for dogs.

But would it work on humans? Louis was about to find out.

In 1885, a local doctor came to Louis and begged him to treat a 9-year-old boy named Joseph Meister, who had been bitten

When Abraham Lincoln's eldest son, Robert, was bitten by their family dog in 1849, the future president of the United States reportedly took him to the town of Terre Haute in Indiana to receive treatment with a madstone. By then, bite victims from all over the Midwest were traveling there for this unusual "cure." Robert went on to live a very long life, so it's unlikely the Lincolns' dog had rabies, since madstones were later proven to be useless.

savagely by a rabid dog. Although Louis was worried about using his vaccine on a human for the first time, he knew that little Joseph would die without his help because rabies is nearly always fatal. So, two days after the attack, Louis gave the boy the first of fourteen daily injections. Much to his relief, the vaccine worked, and Joseph never developed rabies.

News quickly spread, and soon patients from all over the world were traveling to Paris for Louis's help. By the time he died in 1895, he had treated some twenty thousand people with his rabies vaccine, and fewer than a hundred of those had died. (One of the dead was an Englishman who spent all his time in Paris getting drunk and missed one of his injections because he fell into the river.)

A grateful world, inspired by Louis's achievements, sent donations of money to the Pasteur Institute, which had officially opened in Paris in 1888. Joseph Meister eventually became a caretaker there, until his death in 1940.

Over the next century, scientists continued to improve on Louis's vaccine. In time, they were able to reduce the number of injections a person needs to just four. Nowadays, people can get vaccinated before they are exposed to the rabies virus or just after—as long as they are not showing any symptoms. This is unusual among vaccines because most are only effective before exposure to a virus, not after.

We've learned much more about rabies itself too. It turns out that the Roman writer Celsus, and other people in the ancient world, were right when they said that the disease is carried in the saliva of an infected animal. We also now know that the virus presents itself in two ways. Most people who've been bitten by a rabid animal will develop something called "furious rabies," which causes nervous behavior and fear of water. Left untreated, someone with this form of rabies will die within days of symptoms appearing. The other, less common version is called "paralytic [parra-lit-ick] rabies." Those with this form might not get sick for months or even years after they are bitten. Eventually, the virus reaches the brain, and the patient falls into a coma before dying.

Today, rabies is still a problem, especially in developing countries with poor public health programs and limited access to vaccines. In India alone, it kills around twenty thousand people each year. It's one of the world's most deadly viruses, and almost all who die from it are unvaccinated.

BILLS OF MORTALITY

Famous Deaths from Rabies

1868: Giuseppe Abbati, Italian Artist

Giuseppe was a great artist, who was taught to paint by his dad, as well as at a school in Venice. Later, he became a leading figure in a group of artists in Florence. But he was a very unlucky guy and lost his right eye in a battle while fighting for Italy. Six years later, he was captured at another battle and was imprisoned for a while. Later, while staying at the country home of one of his best customers, he was bitten by his own dog, Cennino, who was suffering from rabies. He spent nearly six weeks in the hospital before he died at the age of thirty-two.

1874: Ada Clare, Actress and Writer

After her only novel was slammed by critics, Ada returned to her former career as an actress. While visiting her agent in New York, she was bitten on the face by his rabid dog, whose teeth sank so deeply into her nose that his jaws had to be pried open. Later, Ada was performing onstage when she began to act very strangely, prompting others to remove her from the theater. She died soon after at the age of thirty-nine.

1849: Edgar Allan Poe, Writer

The famous author was once found lying in the street in Baltimore, Maryland. Since Edgar was known to be a heavy drinker, people just thought he was drunk. But present-day doctors at the University of Maryland have suggested that he might have been suffering from rabies. It was reported that Edgar had great difficulty swallowing water, slipped in and out of consciousness, saw things that weren't really there, and had periods of madness before he fell into a coma and died. Could he have been bitten by a rabid animal?

1887: Hayes St. Leger, 4th Viscount Doneraile

Hayes was an Irish lord, and one of the great huntsmen of his age. One day, he came across some local people who had unearthed a fox cub. He asked if he could keep it. They agreed, and he reared the fox as his pet, taking it everywhere as his mascot. Unfortunately, the fox caught rabies, and in January 1887, it bit Hayes and his coachman. The two men traveled to Paris to visit Louis Pasteur, who by then was well-known for his rabies vaccine. After receiving treatment, they returned to Ireland, where the coachman recovered, but Hayes grew sicker and eventually died. It was rumored that his servants suffocated him with pillows to end his suffering and stop him from spreading the disease.

1951: Fernando Poe Sr., Actor and Director

This other famous fella called Poe was a beloved actor and director from the Philippines. He and three of his children were reportedly bitten by a puppy in August 1951. The children all received anti-rabies treatment, but Fernando didn't think he needed it.

Shortly after he finished filming a new movie in October, he began experiencing hip pains and difficulty breathing, which he thought was due to an injury from a fall. But his doctors revealed he was suffering from rabies, and he died shortly before midnight on October 23, a month before his thirty-fifth birthday.

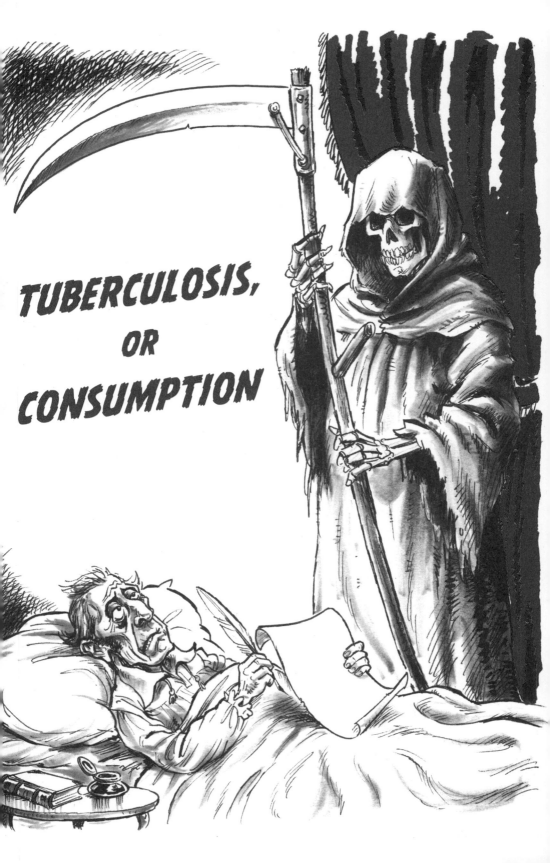

GLENWOOD SPRINGS, COLORADO: NOVEMBER 1887

A man lies sick in bed. He is dangerously thin and so pale that even his ash-blond mustache looks dark against his bony face. He's been delirious with fever for over a month. He's staring down a disease that has been stalking him his entire life. Looking at him now, a stranger would never guess that he was once a tough and feared gunslinger, a legend of the Wild West.

This sharpshooter's name is John Henry Holliday, but he's better known to the world as "Doc" Holliday. His love of gambling and his itchy trigger finger have made him famous. In coming years, countless books will be written about Doc, and movie stars will play him in Westerns. But here and now—as he lies in a cramped bedroom coughing up blood—fate isn't giving him a Hollywood ending.

Doc's eventful life began in Georgia, far from the lawless frontier where it will end. When he was fifteen, his mother died of tuberculosis [tew-bur-cue-low-siss]—a disease so common at this time that it kills one in seven people in the United States. It works itself deep into the lungs and causes terrible coughing fits, fevers, chills, and weight loss. Tuberculosis sets in motion a slow death with no known cure.

After his mom died, Doc was determined to make the best of life, and he went to dental school in Philadelphia. He later set up a practice in Atlanta, Georgia. When he developed a nagging cough, he paid a visit to

DOC HOLLIDAY

his uncle, who also happened to be a doctor. Doc's uncle diagnosed him with tuberculosis and told him that he didn't have long to live. So, Doc headed out west for a "change of air," which he hoped might help.

On his travels, he got to know the tough gambler and lawman Wyatt Earp. Wyatt was based in Tombstone, Arizona, which was quickly becoming one of the richest mining towns in the country thanks to the discovery of silver in the area. Wyatt and his brothers policed Tombstone with an iron fist. Trouble was brewing with a local gang of outlaws who called themselves the Cowboys. Based on a ranch on the outskirts of the town, the Cowboys were made up of thieves, cattle rustlers, and killers. They wanted to get rid of the Earp boys and control Tombstone themselves. By 1881, a showdown was in the cards.

One afternoon, Doc and Wyatt noticed five of the Cowboys near the O.K. Corral. This was a pen for horses, named after its onetime owner, Old Kindersley. What happened next lasted just thirty seconds, but writers and movie studios will eventually make it the most famous gunfight in the history of the Old West.

Wyatt's brother, Virgil, might have fired the first shot, putting a bullet in a gang member's chest. As other triggers were pulled, Doc hit one

of the Cowboys with a shotgun blast, and Wyatt wounded another in the stomach. When it was all over, the outlaws who hadn't been killed ran for their lives, while Wyatt's brothers, and Doc himself, were left bleeding.

Around thirty shots had been fired altogether. Doc and the Earps were charged with murder but later were found not guilty.

Doc's injuries healed, and he and Wyatt rode together for a lot of years afterward, often falling into bloody gun battles with other outlaws. But Doc's tuberculosis grew worse and worse, until he eventually headed out alone to Colorado. There, he checked himself into a hotel in Glenwood Springs, a favored spot for those suffering with tuberculosis. In fact, so popular is the state among the sick that one in three people living there have TB. They all hope that the dry mountain air will ease their symptoms.

But right now, on this November morning, all the minerals and vapors bubbling out of the rocks can do nothing to help poor Doc. He wakes up and asks for a glass of whiskey. He knows that the end has come. Perhaps he always thought he'd die with his boots on, because, noticing his bare feet, his last words are, "Well, I'll be d*%#@d! This is funny!"

He dies, at the age of just thirty-six, and passes into legend.

TUBERCULOSIS HAS HAD MANY weird, wonderful, and unpronounceable names over the centuries.

The ancient Greeks called it "phthisis" [thigh-sis], while the ancient Romans called it "tabes" [tay-bees]. In the nineteenth century, it was known to Europeans as the "white plague" because it made patients very pale and very thin. It was also known as "consumption," since it seemed to slowly consume people.

Patients themselves were often called "lungers" because they had a deep, raspy cough caused by the lumpy growths that filled their lungs. In 1679, a Dutch doctor by the name of Franciscus

Sylvius gave these growths the fancy Latin name "*tubercula glandulosa*," or "tubercles." But it wasn't until 1834 that a German doctor called Johann Schönlein named the disease "tuberculosis." Today, it's often shortened to "TB."

So, now that we've cleared that up, let's get on with the story of this grim sickness that has plagued the world for a very long time.

TB is certainly one of history's deadliest diseases. It has killed more than a BILLION people in the past two hundred years alone! But it has been troubling humankind for much longer than that. Scientists think it first started infecting people in the Stone Age, around nine thousand years ago. Signs of tuberculosis have been found in human remains everywhere, from ancient Israel to

In 1914, a man named Gavrilo Princip [Gav-rillo Prin-sip] wanted to free his country, Bosnia, from the rule of a European emperor. Gavrilo was dying from TB and felt he had nothing to lose. So, when the emperor's heir, Archduke Franz Ferdinand, was visiting the city of Sarajevo, Gavrilo fired a revolver into his car and killed him and his wife. For a whole bunch of confusing and boring reasons that historians still argue about, this murder threw Europe into total chaos and began the First World War. It lasted four long years and caused twenty million deaths. Gavrilo was imprisoned, and later, because the tuberculosis had spread to his bones, he had to have his arm amputated. He died just months before the end of the war that he had helped start.

ancient Egypt and beyond. And it's mentioned in writings from ancient Greece, India, and China.

For nearly all of history, TB wasn't properly understood—like most of the diseases in this book. Many doctors thought it passed from parent to child because entire families commonly fell sick with it. Doctors couldn't offer any helpful treatments, either. Often their advice was just to eat healthy food, rest a lot, and get plenty of fresh air.

From the Middle Ages, the French and the English believed their kings and queens had special powers to cure TB with a simple tap of the hand. This was known as "the King's Touch" (even if it was the queen performing the task). In the seventeenth century,

King Charles II, who must have been like some kind of royal octopus, touched more than ninety thousand British sufferers! The practice died out around 1712, but the disease itself continued to spread like peanut butter on a hot day.

Although TB was most common among poorer people living in crowded conditions and working tough jobs, it gained a reputation as a "romantic" disease because it also affected a number of famous writers and artists in the nineteenth century. The poet John Keats famously died from it in 1821. During this time, creative genius became closely linked with TB. The disease was thought to fuel writers like Robert Louis Stevenson (who wrote *The Strange Case of Dr. Jekyll and Mr. Hyde*) even as it "consumed" them.

Some people believed that TB's high fevers could power creative energy. Others thought that the enforced downtime gave artists a chance to think up great ideas. Whatever the reasoning, many people wanted to get TB in

the Victorian period—even though it often ended in death. Women even used makeup to make themselves look pale and frail, like TB patients. Imagine how much worse it would've been if TikTok had been a thing back then!

During this time, infections around the globe exploded, and

millions of people died each year. Hospitals overflowed with TB patients. In New York City, a ferry had to be turned into a make-shift ward. Many doctors were so desperate to find a cure, they were willing to try just about anything. Some had their patients inhale poisonous vapors of hemlock, swallow a remedy made from moss, rub vinegar onto their chests, chug cod liver oil, or even slather myrrh (a sticky resin) all over their bodies.

In the 1880s, an Italian doctor named Carlo Forlanini came up with an even more extreme solution. He thought the best thing for patients' lungs was to rest them, because the very act of breathing was making the diseased tubercles inside the lungs bigger. His

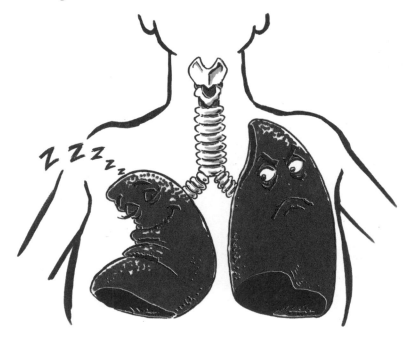

solution? Collapse a lung! He took big old syringes full of nitrogen, stuck them into the space between the ribs and the lung, and pumped the gas inside. This would push on the lung, making it collapse. Perhaps the wildest thing about it was that it actually worked! The technique became the first partly successful treatment for TB. But walking around with a floppy, useless lung inside your rib cage is far from ideal. So, doctors kept looking for better solutions.

In the meantime, the best that doctors could do for their patients was to make them comfortable. Concern that the disease might be contagious meant many patients were taken out of their homes to protect their families from catching it. In the early nineteenth century, the first special hospitals for TB patients, called "sanatoriums," appeared.

Patients in sanatoriums were usually confined to bed, with no kind of fun allowed. To stop them from losing weight, they were

N-n-nurse, my raw eggs have frozen . . .

fed special diets, which could include six glasses of milk and six raw eggs every day. And they were given plenty of fresh air. In fact, the buildings often had "sleeping porches" where patients would spend their nights outdoors, even in the bitter cold.

In America, TB patients like Doc Holliday headed to the newly opened-up west. From the early 1800s, people in the States began moving farther westward, into the lands of Native Americans who had already been there for a very long time. With its big skies, broad plains, and mountain air, it seemed like an ideal place to get well. In fact, the city of Pasadena in California started out as a colony for TB patients from Indiana. Word spread that the Californian climate was great for the sick. But finding a place for all these newcomers became a real problem. Not everyone could afford to be in a sanatorium, and poorer people were thrown together in crowded areas, which led to the further spread of TB.

On the opposite coast, a doctor named Edward Trudeau set up a sanatorium at Saranac Lake, New York, in 1884. It offered treatment to poorer patients at a really low cost. Edward and many of the other staff members suffered from TB themselves. Many of them worked at the sanatorium without pay. Edward also built the country's first major institute for the study of TB. Sadly, both he and his daughter died of the disease, but Edward had started a trend. Soon, sanatoriums popped up all over the United States. By 1925, there were hundreds of thousands of beds available for patients across the nation.

As with all diseases, the key to curing TB was first to understand what was causing it. And as early as 1720, a clever Englishman named Benjamin Marten came close to nailing it.

Benjamin suggested that there were tiny little creatures that invaded people's bodies and made them sick. Today, we would call these "germs"—though it would take another hundred and fifty years before doctors would begin to understand them. Benjamin also suspected that a healthy person lying in bed next to someone with TB would become ill by drawing the sick person's breath into their own lungs. The trouble was that everyone thought it was a silly idea. "Invisible creatures, killing our patients?! Hogwash! Poppycock!! BALDERDASH!!" they cried (or something like that—we're guessing, to be honest).

Nearly a century later, a French doctor by the name of René Laennec [Run-nay Len-eck] figured out something interesting by dissecting the dead bodies of those who had died from TB. This was that patients could develop the disease's tell-tale "tubercles" in parts of the body other than the lungs.

René also invented a medical instrument that would change the way doctors diagnosed patients forever. As a musician, he carved his own flutes, and he used his woodworking skills to create a special tube. He put one end of it to a patient's chest, while listening at the other end for sounds from the heart or from lungs riddled with tuberculosis. He had invented the first stethoscope, a device still essential to doctors today. But sadly, René

died of TB himself in 1826. He likely caught it from one of the many patients whose lives he had tried to save.

Then, a breakthrough happened in 1882. The German scientist Robert Koch discovered rod-shaped bacteria in patients suffering from TB. Although the scientist Louis Pasteur had already figured out that germs cause disease, Robert was the first scientist to link particular bacteria to particular diseases. He was able to prove beyond doubt what Benjamin Marten had suspected way back in 1720: tuberculosis *is* caused by a tiny living creature!

ROBERT KOCH

In 1905, Robert Koch was given a major award called a Nobel Prize for his amazing work on tuberculosis.

Once scientists understood that TB was caused by a germ, they got busy trying to make a vaccine. Two French scientists worked on the problem at the Pasteur Institute, using similar techniques that Louis Pasteur himself had used to create the rabies vaccine. In 1921, after many years of work, they tested their vaccine on their first human patient, and within a few years, it was clear that they had done the world a humungous favor by creating the first TB vaccine. It was named the Bacille Calmette-Guérin vaccine after them, or "BCG" for short. From then on, huge vaccination drives began across the globe.

The BCG vaccine is very effective against the worst and rarest forms of TB (the deadly ones), and it's especially good at protecting babies and kids from these. But it's less good at stopping people from getting the version that attacks the lungs. Since vaccines were not a "magic bullet" cure,

Spitting used to be a big (and disgusting!) problem in nineteenth-century America. People did it absolutely everywhere because they had a lot of spittle from chewing tobacco or from phlegm caused by TB. Many public places had spittoons, which were metal or pottery containers into which people could spit their loogies. But public health officials were worried that spitting might be spreading tuberculosis. So, they began to ban spitting in public spaces, first in New York in 1896, and then in nearly a hundred fifty other US cities. In some places, the practice is still outlawed today!

doctors and scientists also worked on making drugs that could treat the symptoms of tuberculosis.

Alexander Fleming had shown the world the bacteria-bashing abilities of the mold penicillin in 1929, and this changed the way doctors treated many infections. Unfortunately, it turned out that this wonder drug was useless when it came to treating TB. But a

Jewish Russian–American scientist named Selman Waksman felt sure that some other kind of mold could work. To find out, he and his research team looked at a bunch of microbes found in soil. In 1943, they discovered one that became known as streptomycin.

This was the cure that could finally kick TB's skinny butt. During his career, Waksman discovered more than fifteen "antibiotics"—a word he coined for medicines that could kill bacteria. And here's another fun fact: streptomycin can also cure bubonic plague!

As science began to unlock the mysteries of TB, doctors started having doubts about how useful all those freezing cold sanatoriums actually were. So, they set up an experiment in India to see if treating patients with anti-TB drugs in a sanatorium was any better than treating them with the same drugs in their homes. The volunteers were studied over the course of five years, and it turned out that where they were treated made no difference whatsoever. It also became clear that once a patient began treatment, the risk of their families catching TB was lowered. The end of sanatoriums was now in sight.

But it wasn't the end of tuberculosis. Sadly, some ten million people still fall ill with the disease each year—more than all the people living in New York City. Of those, around 1.5 million die from it. So, it's still a problem. But we're a heck of a lot better at dealing with TB today than back when Doc Holliday was gasping for his last breath without his boots on.

BILLS OF MORTALITY

Famous Deaths from Tuberculosis

1553: Edward VI, King of England

Edward was only nine years old when he was crowned king of England, but he didn't reign for long. He once caught malaria, and he got measles, which left him weak and at risk from other sicknesses. Sure enough, he caught tuberculosis, which gave him a terrible cough, multicolored phlegm, and sores all over his body. He died when he was only fifteen years old. People in the past might have believed kings and queens could cure their TB, but that clearly didn't stop them from getting it themselves!

1642: Armand Jean du Plessis, Cardinal Richelieu

If you've ever read *The Three Musketeers,* or seen one of the film versions, you'll have heard of Cardinal Richelieu [Reesh-ull-yur]. He was as powerful a statesman and churchman in real life as he is in fiction, and he rose to be the French king's chief minister. He was clever and ruthless, with a network of spies across Europe. But his health failed, and he suffered from migraines, a blocked bladder, fevers, and tuberculosis of the bowels. He eventually died aged fifty-seven. When revolution swept over France in 1789, his well-preserved head was stolen and put on display. In 1866, it was finally reunited with his body—and they have stayed together happily ever since.

1817: Jane Austen, Writer

Jane was an English author who wrote many well-loved stories about life, love, and marriage among the wealthier people of her time. Film directors just can't stop themselves from turning her books into movies, even if you ask them very politely. Jane's death at the age of forty-one has been blamed on a rare sickness of the glands called Addison's disease, but some experts think a more likely cause was TB that she caught from drinking unsafe, unpasteurized milk (as Louis Pasteur hadn't invented pasteurization yet).

1845: Andrew Jackson, Seventh President of the United States

Andrew was a grumpy guy with a knack for cheating death. As a prisoner during the Revolutionary War, he was slashed with a sword when he refused to clean a British soldier's boots. He fought a lot of duels, taking bullets to the chest, one of which stayed there for the rest of his life. When he became president of the United States, someone tried to shoot him, but the guns misfired, and Andrew charged at the attacker with his cane. His luck ran out when he was seventy-eight, and he died of tuberculosis and heart failure.

1962: Eleanor Roosevelt, First Lady of the United States

Eleanor's husband, President Franklin D. Roosevelt, served four terms in office, making her history's longest-serving First Lady. She was a brilliant and powerful woman, famous for her political skills and her defense of the rights of African Americans. But there are arguments about the cause of her death at the age of seventy-eight. Some experts think that her doctors failed to notice that she had miliary tuberculosis, a form of TB in which large numbers of bacteria travel through the bloodstream, spreading the disease to various parts of the body. The mystery may never be solved.

NEW YORK CITY: THE SUMMER OF 1832

The city is filthier than it has ever been. Rotting garbage and manure fill the streets. Living conditions for many New Yorkers are growing ever more crowded as people from all over the world flock to America seeking opportunity. In such a place, the threat of disease has always loomed. And, sure enough, a new sickness is now on the loose.

It began in India and spread west with ships as they docked in ports across the globe. By the summer of 1832, it had arrived in Canada, making its way south down the Hudson River and into the heart of New York City.

As the disease quickly spreads through the winding roads and alleyways, those who can afford second homes flee to the countryside in panic. But many of the poor—like the Irish immigrants and African Americans—have nowhere to go. They are crammed into an area known as Five Points in lower Manhattan, where cholera can spread freely among them in their overcrowded slums. And it does. Just as people in the fourteenth century blamed those with leprosy for spreading plague, many wealthy people are now blaming the cholera outbreak on the poor themselves, claiming it is a punishment for their "sinful" lives. But the rich soon eat their words as the sickness finds its way into their swanky neighborhoods too.

Cholera is a grim disease that causes painful cramps, diarrhea, puking, and raging thirst. It can kill within hours of these symptoms appearing.

Doctors don't have any idea how to treat it, so they prescribe many use-less remedies, some of which contain a highly addictive drug called opium.

They also have no clue what causes cholera. Their best guess is our old friend "miasma," which they believe is seeping from the trash and poop rotting in the streets.

As hospitals become overrun with patients, temporary medical stations have to be built in places like empty schools and banks. Meanwhile, people turn their hatred on those trying to help the sick. Rumors spread that the doctors themselves are killing patients and using the corpses for dissection to teach anatomy to medical students! Sadly, the reality is that those trying their hardest to help the sick often fall victim to cholera themselves, and die.

The city's leaders are slow to react to the crisis. When they finally do, they try to fight the outbreak by cleaning up the streets for the first time in decades and sprinkling them with a powerful chemical called quicklime. They also put ships into quarantine and hand out leaflets that explain how they think cholera can best be avoided. Many of the poorer people in New York are moved out of the slums and placed into

temporary housing. These measures can be great at combating disease, but in this case, they come too late to do much good. By the time cholera finally disappears that autumn, it has claimed the lives of thirty-five hundred New Yorkers.

And it will not be the last time that the disease causes this kind of devastation in the world.

CHOLERA IS A REALLY nasty infection of the bowels. Its name likely comes from an ancient Greek word for "bile," which was the fluid in the body that people linked to puking and diarrhea, back when the theory of the four humors was popular. But the word also meant "gutter" and might have been used for the disease because, when you get it, fluids shoot out of you like rainwater out of a gutter. Yikes!

Cholera is sometimes called the "Blue Death" because it can turn your skin a light shade of blue. How does this happen? Well, it's a bit complicated.

When someone is puking and pooping endlessly due to cholera, they can lose up to a quart of water from their body each hour, causing them to shed half their body weight in a single day! This is dangerous because an adult human body is made up of 55 to 60 percent water, and that water is crucial to many of its functions. It allows you to digest food and control your temperature. It even helps your brain work. One consequence of rapid water loss, or "dehydration," caused by cholera is that your blood becomes thick in your veins, and it can't carry oxygen around your body effectively. As a result, you turn blue. Unfortunately, once this happens, death is quick to follow.

Most people infected with cholera don't show any symptoms at first, though the germ that causes it can show up in their poop for several days and may infect other people during this time. It takes

In the nineteenth century, human poop was often called "night soil," and the workers who were paid to take it away after dark were known as "night soil men." It was a disgusting, stinky job, as we're sure you can imagine. The night soil men had to pull carts full of waste through the streets as they went from house to house collecting it. They often sold it to farmers, who then used it as fertilizer. Nothing was wasted in the past—not even the waste!

anything from a few hours to several days for someone to feel sick after swallowing food or water contaminated with cholera. Some people get only slightly sick, but if it really takes hold, the disease is deadly when left untreated.

Like many other diseases, nobody understood how cholera was spread when it first appeared on the world's stage. And although there are historical records of disease that sound a lot like cholera, it's impossible to say for sure if they actually were. But there's a description of something that was very possibly cholera breaking out in India in the 1540s.

Later, the first known cholera pandemic began in India's Ganges Delta, with an outbreak in Jessore in 1817. This seems to have been caused by contaminated rice. The disease quickly spread around the globe along land and sea routes. There have been seven major cholera pandemics over the last two hundred years that have killed millions of people across the globe.

There was no shortage of things to worry about for those living through cholera outbreaks in the early and mid-nineteenth century. Because a cholera sufferer might appear dead before they were actually dead, people began to worry about being buried alive. This led to the creation of so-called safety coffins, which were designed to ensure you could safely escape if you found yourself accidentally six feet under!

In 1822, Dr. Adolf Gutsmuth set out to conquer his fear of being buried alive by testing a safety coffin that he had designed. He had himself buried in it and stayed underground for several hours, during which time he enjoyed a meal of soup, sausages, and beer—all delivered to him through a handy feeding tube built into his coffin.

The Germans were especially ingenious when it came to safety coffins, and we know of over

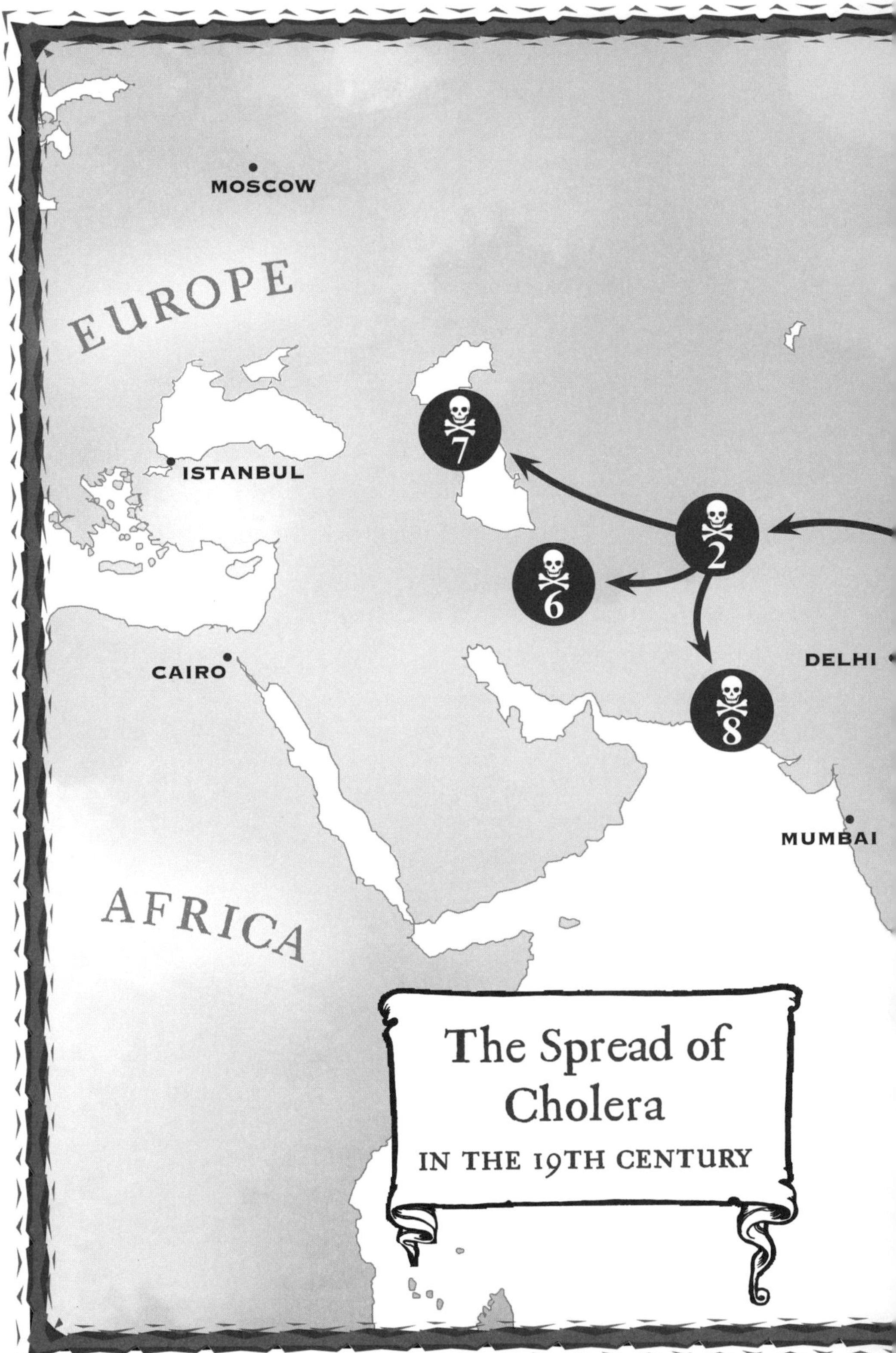

MOSCOW

EUROPE

ISTANBUL

CAIRO

AFRICA

DELHI

MUMBAI

7

2

6

8

The Spread of
Cholera
IN THE 19TH CENTURY

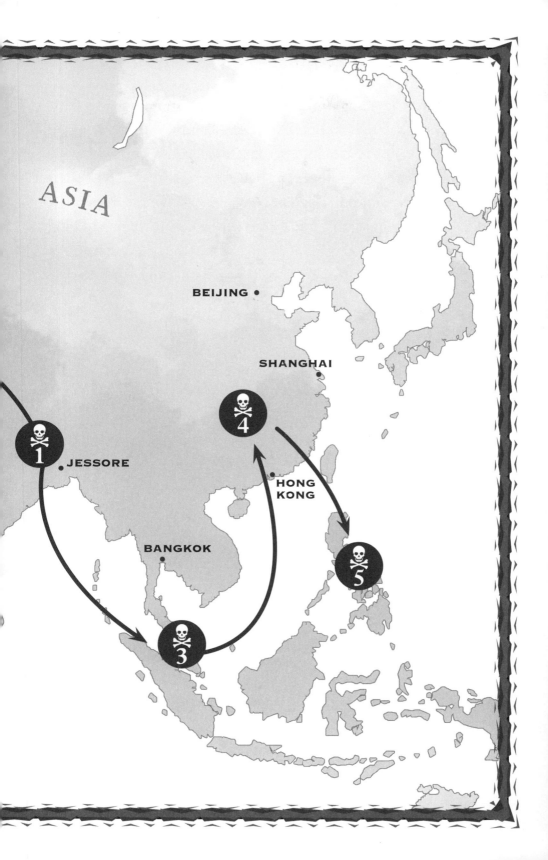

thirty different designs from the nineteenth century. The best-known one was the brainchild of Dr. Johann Gottfried Taberger, which included a system of ropes that attached the corpse's hands, feet, and head to an aboveground bell. Although many later designs tried to incorporate this gizmo, it was by and large a design failure. What Johann didn't factor in is that a corpse begins to bloat and swell as it rots, causing it to shift inside the coffin. These tiny movements would have set the bells ringing . . . and visitors to the graveyard running!

During cholera outbreaks, like the one in New York in 1832, city leaders wanted to introduce local measures that would stop the disease in its tracks. But what should those measures be? The prevention of cholera became part of a much bigger medical argument during this time.

On one side were those who stuck with the old belief that diseases were caused by miasma—or tiny bits of decaying, poisonous, stinky matter in the air. In their minds, the fact that people living in cleaner, less populated neighborhoods tended to get sick less often backed up their beliefs. Believers of miasma theory called for better sanitation, such as airing out public buildings and clearing the streets of foul-smelling waste, which they thought was a source of the miasma. They also encouraged people to wear masks that contained vapors of vinegar or camphor (a chemical from a tree), which they believed would neutralize the smelly miasma.

On the other side of the debate were those who thought diseases were caused by contagion and passed from person to person through physical contact. To them, contagion explained why those who cared for the sick often got ill too. They wanted to limit people's movements and use quarantine to ensure that healthy people didn't come into contact with the sick.

It turns out that neither camp was totally right. Cholera *is* contagious—although it was unclear how the disease was actually infecting people, since germs were not yet understood. And in the 1850s, miasma theory took a couple of hard knocks.

A doctor in London named John Snow turned into a kind of medical Sherlock Holmes when cholera broke out in a neighborhood near his home in 1854. As cases sprang up, he started plotting them on a map. That was when he noticed a pattern forming. Most of those who fell ill were drawing their water from a pump on Broad Street. Even cases that at first glance weren't connected with the pump actually turned out to be. For example, there was a woman who lived quite far away, but she preferred the taste of

the water from the Broad Street pump to water from her own area. She had died two days after drinking from the Broad Street supply.

By his simple but brilliant detective work, John proved that cholera spread through contaminated water supplies, and had nothing to do with poisonous miasma in the air. However, when he published his map to support his ideas, not many people paid attention. But he was able to convince local authorities to remove the handle from the Broad Street pump so people could no longer draw water from it. After that, the outbreak quickly ended.

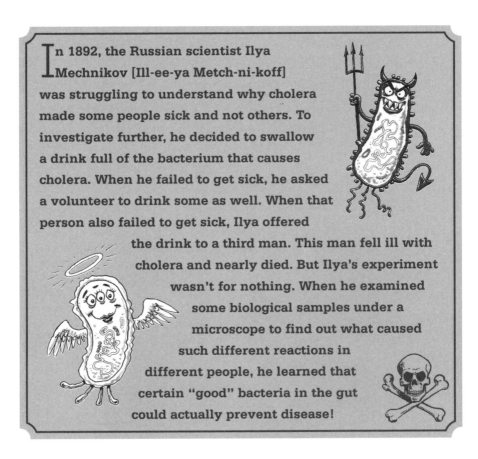

In 1892, the Russian scientist Ilya Mechnikov [Ill-ee-ya Metch-ni-koff] was struggling to understand why cholera made some people sick and not others. To investigate further, he decided to swallow a drink full of the bacterium that causes cholera. When he failed to get sick, he asked a volunteer to drink some as well. When that person also failed to get sick, Ilya offered the drink to a third man. This man fell ill with cholera and nearly died. But Ilya's experiment wasn't for nothing. When he examined some biological samples under a microscope to find out what caused such different reactions in different people, he learned that certain "good" bacteria in the gut could actually prevent disease!

Later, it was discovered that the pump drew water from a well dug only a few feet from a cesspit full of human poop. The diaper of a baby who had caught cholera from another source had wound up in that cesspit, infecting the well water and causing a widespread outbreak.

In 1858, John died after suffering a stroke. Like so many doctors and scientists, he didn't live to see his theories accepted. Today, he is now considered a pioneer in the field of public health and epidemiology [eppy-deemy-ollo-gee], which is the study of how often diseases occur in different groups of people and why. Although John's findings weren't recognized immediately, they did eventually bring about changes in public health, like the construction of better water systems and sewers.

But before such improvements, and just a few weeks after John's death, a terrible stench bubbled up in London, creeping into every street, alley, and courtyard within a mile of the River Thames. The scorching summer heat made the terrible smell even worse. People went out of their way to avoid going near the river.

"The Great Stink," as it became known, was due to huge amounts of human waste piled along the riverbanks—a problem that had been growing worse as London became more and more populated. The smell was so bad that government officials in parliament had to cover their windows with heavy cloth just so they could continue working. Thousands fled the city in fear for their lives.

And yet, strangely, no epidemics sprang up that summer. People (especially those who believed in miasma) wondered how this could be. If only they had paid more attention to John Snow's theories!

Toward the end of the nineteenth century, discoveries by brilliant scientists like Louis Pasteur helped explain why both bad stuff floating in the air *and* contact between a sick and healthy person could cause illness. It all came down to germs.

> Before diseases like cholera could be treated effectively, ships with sick people aboard had to anchor offshore. To show that they were in quarantine, they flew a yellow flag known as the "yellow jack."

Do you remember Robert Koch, the famous German scientist who discovered the tuberculosis bacterium in 1882? Well, for a long time he was also credited with discovering the bacterium that caused cholera. A year after his breakthrough with TB, Robert traveled to India, which was in the grip of a cholera outbreak. By studying samples from the bowels of people who died of the disease, he was able to identify the cholera bacterium. Robert was widely praised for his important work, which marked the beginning of the end of old ideas about miasma.

In reality, an Italian scientist named Filippo Pacini had first identified the cause of cholera, though he wasn't credited with his discovery until eighty-two years after his death. Filippo had turned down a career in the church to take up medicine and soon became a big fan of microscopes. He rose to the top of the medical school in the University of Florence. When cholera hit the city in 1854, he got to work trying to understand the disease.

FILIPPO PACINI

Using his microscope, Filippo looked at samples from the bowels of cholera victims and found the same bacteria that Robert Koch would find all those years later. Filippo published a report about his discovery. He kept studying cholera and even recommended the very sensible remedy of getting fluids back into a patient's dehydrated body. But his work was completely ignored, and most of his peers clung to the idea that miasma was to blame.

In 1965, Filippo's findings were finally recognized. Nowadays, it is the Italian scientist and not the much more famous Robert Koch who is hailed as the true discoverer of the cholera bacterium.

In fact, the germ was eventually renamed *Vibrio cholerae Pacini* in his honor.

Sadly, the world isn't rid of cholera just yet. Millions still fall sick with it each year. But people with really bad cases can often be treated with antibiotics. And—just as Filippo suggested 170 years ago—rehydration, or replacing lost fluids, is now the main treatment for cholera.

Perhaps the best thing to come out of cholera epidemics is that they forced the world to grab a mop and bucket and finally clean up its act!

BILLS OF MORTALITY

Famous Deaths from Cholera

1690: Cristóbal of Saint Catherine

When he was seven, Cristóbal ran away from home to join a monastery, but his brothers caught him and brought him back home. Later, he worked in a Christian hospital and then became a priest to the Spanish army fighting in Portugal. Eventually, he became a monk, and in 1673, Cristóbal founded his own Franciscan order in the Spanish city of Córdoba. He died of cholera, which he caught while caring for the sick during an epidemic. He was made a saint in 2013.

1831: Duke Konstantin Pavlovich Romanov of Russia

In 1825, Konstantin was supposed to become the ruler of Russia. But he announced he didn't want to. This was because he had divorced his first wife and married a Polish noblewoman named Joanna. Konstantin's family, the Romanovs, thought that Joanna wasn't good enough for him, and that any kids she had wouldn't be royal enough to take the throne. So, Konstantin's younger brother became ruler instead. Konstantin still performed his royal duties, though, and fought in the Napoleonic wars. He even survived an assassination attempt and became commander-in-chief of the Polish army. But he caught cholera while on his travels and died soon afterward.

1836: Charles X, King of France

In his younger days, Charles was close to his sister-in-law, the notorious queen Marie Antoinette, who was beheaded during the French Revolution. She once had a bet with Charles that his new castle couldn't be built within three months. But it was! Charles later became king, but he was kicked off the throne in 1830. After that, he left France and set out for the Mediterranean coast. But when he arrived in Görz in the Kingdom of Illyria, he caught cholera and died. As a mark of respect, the townsfolk draped their windows in black cloth. Charles was laid to rest in a monastery in what is now Slovenia, and he's the only king of France buried outside his homeland.

1849: Hester Lane, Abolitionist and Anti-Slavery Campaigner

Hester was born into slavery in Maryland, but by the 1820s, she was a free woman running a successful decorating business in New York. Over the course of her lifetime, she took a lot of risks by traveling south to buy the freedom of enslaved people. She also raised funds for the campaign to end slavery. In 1849, sick passengers on a ship that had been quarantined at New York's Staten Island escaped. Soon after, an outbreak of cholera hit the city, killing over five thousand people, including Hester.

1850: Zachary Taylor, President of the United States

On Independence Day in 1850, President Taylor was hot and bothered after enjoying the celebrations in Washington, DC. He took a stroll along the Potomac River and then returned to the White House, where he drank iced water and ate some cherries. Soon after, he was hit with a really bad bellyache. His doctors diagnosed him with cholera, and four days later, he was dead. Not every-one believed that he died of natural causes, however, and rumors swept the country that the president may have been poisoned by his political enemies. This was disproved in the 1990s, though, when scientists dug up Taylor's body and tested it. They found small amounts of arsenic in his system, but no more than would be found naturally in anyone else, and there certainly wasn't enough to kill the former president.

SCURVY, OR THE PLAGUE OF THE SEA

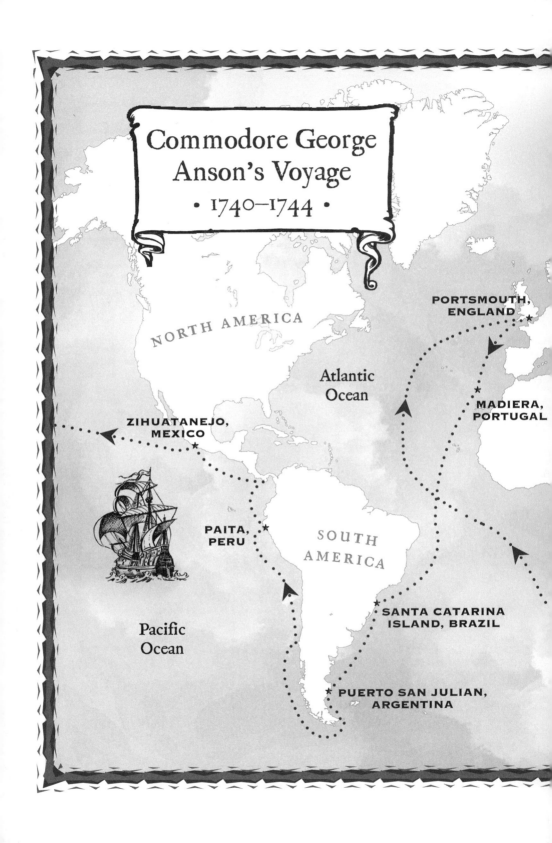

Commodore George Anson's Voyage
• 1740–1744 •

NORTH AMERICA

PORTSMOUTH, ENGLAND

Atlantic Ocean

MADIERA, PORTUGAL

ZIHUATANEJO, MEXICO

PAITA, PERU

SOUTH AMERICA

Pacific Ocean

SANTA CATARINA ISLAND, BRAZIL

PUERTO SAN JULIAN, ARGENTINA

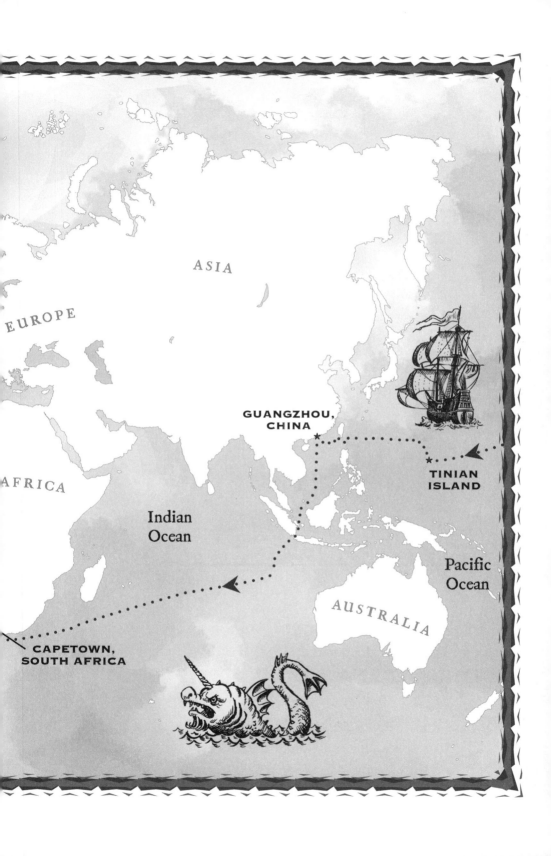

PORTSMOUTH, ENGLAND: SEPTEMBER 1740

England is at war with Spain. The Royal Navy gives Commodore George Anson a squadron of eight wooden ships and orders him to set sail across the Atlantic Ocean toward South America. Part of his mission is to attack and seize Spanish warships, one of which carries huge amounts of treasure between Mexico and the Philippines.

But the voyage is an unlucky one from the very beginning. Many of the crew are old and weak. Delays and constant illness dog the mission. When the ships do eventually cross the ocean, George Anson's chief surgeon and two of his captains die, and eighty sick men have to be put ashore on an island.

Then, as the squadron spends a month sailing around the storm-battered Cape Horn at the tip of South America, the first cases of a mysterious new disease appear. Its victims suffer terrible symptoms for weeks before they die. At first, they become incredibly tired, and they will eventually grow too feeble to move. In time, their joints begin to ache, their gums begin to swell, and their breath begins to stink. Blue or red blotches also appear all over their scaly skin as they start to bleed from the inside.

Perhaps the weirdest thing is that old wounds open up again. One of George's men was injured over fifty years earlier at a battle in Ireland. His scars now split open and look fresh, and a long-healed broken bone

snaps once again. And he isn't the only one suffering. The illness, known as scurvy, kills more than forty men on George's flagship, Centurion, alone.

George turns north toward his squadron's meeting point: the island of Socorro, off the western coast of present-day Mexico. For weeks, his ships battle huge storms. During this time, he also loses roughly six men each day to scurvy. On finally anchoring at Socorro, he waits for the rest of the squadron. When they don't show, he sets sail for the second meeting point of Juan Fernandez Island. Over the next two weeks, George loses another eighty men to scurvy.

The battered squadron eventually gathers at Juan Fernandez, but only four ships have made it. The rest have either sunk or were forced to turn back. By the time the crew has made repairs, seven in ten of the men on board have died—most from scurvy.

The squadron continues on its way, carrying out raids along the South American coast and capturing several Spanish ships. It then heads west, deep into the Pacific Ocean, in search of the enemy's prized treasure galleon. But scurvy returns to claim more victims. George gathers the few surviving men into the Centurion and destroys the other ships as there is not enough crew left to sail them. At least ten men are now dying from scurvy every day. George makes for China, where the sick and exhausted crew stays for a while. The men then set out again and finally manage to capture the galleon they have been chasing. Carrying tons of glittering booty worth £500,000, George and his dwindling crew set sail for England.

After sailing around the globe, the ship arrives home at last in the summer of 1744. Those who have survived the terrible journey have been at sea for four long years. It is celebrated as one of the greatest voyages in British naval history, and George Anson becomes a wealthy and famous hero.

But he had begun his voyage with nearly two thousand men. Only four have died in battle or from injury. A staggering fourteen hundred of them were killed by the puzzling and dreadful scurvy.

BETWEEN THE YEARS 1500 AND 1800, scurvy killed two million sailors. It was the leading cause of death on ships, taking more lives than all other diseases, disasters, and warfare combined. Anyone, from the meanest pirate to the best-dressed admiral, could get it. And it remained a problem into the twentieth century, making life very difficult for polar explorers on long expeditions. For centuries, nobody had a clue what scurvy was, and nobody could agree on how to prevent or cure it.

The story of how the mystery was finally solved will make you want to suck a lemon.

Scurvy plagued the world for thousands of years. It seemed to rear its ugly head whenever food was scarce. The ancient Greeks wrote about it, as did the ancient Egyptians. During the Middle Ages, a bunch of Christian soldiers called Crusaders fell ill with scurvy while fighting in Egypt. When the sickness took hold, dead flesh had to be cut away from the soldiers' swollen gums so that they could chew their food. The Crusaders blamed the disease on the eels that they had been eating, which they thought had become poisonous after feasting on dead bodies floating in a nearby river.

I'm giving up crusaders for Lent.

Scurvy became a much bigger problem for Europeans when improvements to ships allowed sailors to spend months, even years, at sea. In 1497, the Portuguese explorer Vasco da Gama set sail in search of a sea route to the East Indies. When scurvy began to hammer his crew, Vasco ordered them to rinse their teeth and gums with their own pee, which some people thought could cure scurvy. But in spite of turning themselves into actual potty mouths, 100 of the 160 sailors died.

In the 1530s, the French captain Jacques Cartier lost 25 of his men to scurvy on an expedition to North America. Cartier ordered

JACQUES CARTIER

one of the corpses to be cut open in an attempt to understand the disease. Inside the dead man's chest was a withered, white heart

Sailors led hard, dangerous lives. Climbing rigging and pulling on ropes to raise sails was backbreaking. They also lived in dirty, damp, cramped, rat-infested conditions. But perhaps the worst thing was the food.

Supplies had to last a long time, so meat and fish were preserved in salt. Salt-cured pork was tough enough to carve into little works of art. The cheese could get so hard that sailors would shape it into buttons for their clothes. There was also "hardtack," which was basically flour cakes baked so solid that they had to be soaked for ages just to be chewable. Hardtack was usually stale too, and often full of bugs called weevils.

From the 1750s, ships were stocked with "portable soup." This was made from cooked animal guts, vegetables, and salt, which was dried into blocks that had to be boiled before being eaten. There was plenty of booze aboard, though, and sailors were given a gallon of beer each and every day. So, while they were getting a whopping four thousand calories daily, there was very little fresh fruit and vegetables to keep them healthy.

surrounded by dark "water" and black lungs. But what had caused scurvy in the first place remained a mystery. The disease continued to ravage the crew until only three men, including Jacques, were left. When they landed in what is now known as Canada, Jacques spoke with an Indigenous man who recommended a local cure made from the juice of an evergreen tree. Jacques gave the juice to his sick crew, and within a few days, all of them got better. Elsewhere, early European explorers noticed that Native Americans were supplementing their limited winter diet with a tea made from pine needles.

Could this be the key to treating scurvy?

As you'll remember from our journey through the Black Death, many European and American doctors believed in the four humors—black bile, yellow bile, phlegm, and blood. They also thought most diseases arose when these same humors were out of whack. Building on this, a sixteenth-century Dutchman named John Echth [Egg't] put forward the idea that a blockage in the spleen led to a buildup of black bile, which in turn caused scurvy. Although this belief was dead wrong, it caught on and was generally accepted as true until the middle of the eighteenth century.

There were all kinds of "cures" for scurvy. These included bloodletting, drinking seawater, smoking tobacco, and bathing in animal blood. Because the early stages of scurvy caused tiredness that was mistaken for laziness, captains often made sick sailors do extra work. Some pirates believed being buried up to the neck in sand was particularly effective in fighting scurvy. After all, humans are land-dwelling creatures, so it made sense to many people that being back in your natural element would cure an illness of the sea. One sick member of George Anson's rowing party was so convinced that the air on land was healthier than sea air that, when the crew came ashore, he asked his shipmates to dig a hole in the ground and then put his mouth to it so that he could get a good lungful of earthy air.

The navy had given George Anson's crew several of the most popular treatments of the day. These included vinegar, "elixir of vitriol" (a harmful mixture of alcohol and sulfuric acid), and a poisonous medicine called Ward's Drop and Pill, which caused the poops and permanent liver damage without curing anything. It is said to have given one of George Anson's men a nosebleed so bad that he nearly died.

The Royal Navy also recommended fermented barley malt as a remedy. And a British explorer named Captain James Cook became convinced that sauerkraut was the answer. Since his men hated this sour, fermented cabbage, he came up with a clever way to tempt them to eat it: he had it served to his high-ranking officers every day so that the crew would think they were missing out on something special and ask for some too.

Captain Cook wasn't far off the mark. Diet did seem to be

key to warding off scurvy. On the lush island of Juan Fernández, George Anson's men got better after eating a plant called spoonwort. They weren't the first to use it. John Hall, an English doctor in the seventeenth century (and also William Shakespeare's son-in-law) treated scurvy with a drink made by boiling spoonwort and watercress in beer. In fact, so effective was spoonwort at treating symptoms that it was also known as "scurvy grass."

Some people noticed that fruit also seemed to help. In 1617, John Woodall, the surgeon general of a big, global trading business called the East India Company, wrote that citrus fruit, and especially lemons, had a dramatic effect on scurvy victims. And in 1622, the explorer Sir Richard Hawkins wrote that lemons and oranges were a great cure for scurvy, adding that he wished someone really smart would look into what he called "the plague of the sea." Unfortunately, it would take over a hundred years for that to happen.

The naval surgeon James Lind is remembered as the man who helped solve the mystery of scurvy once and for all.

James was fifteen when he began working for a doctor in Edinburgh, Scotland. In 1738, he joined the Royal Navy, a short while

JAMES LIND

before Spain and England went to war. After seven years as a surgeon's mate, he was promoted to surgeon on the ship HMS *Salisbury*. When scurvy struck the crew of this vessel, the captain allowed James to begin an experiment. He took twelve sick men, divided them into six pairs, and gave each pair a different treatment. These were . . .

- A quart of cider a day.
- Two spoonfuls of vinegar, three times a day.
- Twenty-five drops of elixir of vitriol (the alcohol and sulfuric acid mixture mentioned earlier), three times a day.
- Half a pint of seawater a day.
- A paste made of garlic, horse radish, mustard seeds, balsam of Peru (resin from a certain tree), and myrrh (resin from a different tree), three times a day.
- Two oranges and one lemon a day.

By the end of the week, the men who had been given oranges and lemons were well enough to get up and nurse their sick buddies. By carrying out the first known controlled experiment on scurvy, James was able to find a cure. He included his findings in a book that he published in 1753.

So that was the end of scurvy, right? James Lind had saved the day with refreshing slices of zesty goodness! Well, not exactly . . .

The problem was that James didn't make any clear statements about his findings in his book, and the details of how he carried out his experiment were thin. He still didn't understand *why* citrus fruits cured scurvy, and he continued to believe that the disease had many causes that needed many remedies. He spent 450 pages talking about other cures—like exercise and fresh air—which he thought were just as important as citrus fruits when it came to preventing and treating scurvy.

Another problem was that Britain's head medical honchos didn't want to listen to poor James. After all, he was only a lowly ship's surgeon. It wasn't easy for a humble man like him to convince people around him that he was on to something. For the most part, doctors clung to the idea that scurvy was caused by an imbalance in those pesky four humors, and they continued to big-up several largely useless remedies.

It took a determined admirer of James Lind's work to convince the Royal Navy to make real changes. An important naval doc called Gilbert Blane finally persuaded the Admiralty to introduce lemon juice as a regular part of sailors' diets in 1795. Lemons were later replaced with limes because they were easily found in Britain's Caribbean colonies. For this reason, British sailors—and eventually all Brits—became known as "limeys."

Sadly, James died a year before these changes took place. But his vital work on scurvy later earned him the title "Father of Naval Medicine." In his honor, a lemon tree was eventually added to the Institute of Naval Medicine's coat of arms in Britain.

Despite these steps in the right direction, scurvy continued to pose a serious threat to those on both land and sea well into the nineteenth century. It was especially bad during the American Civil War since it was difficult to get fresh food to troops

Driven by desperation and hunger, some sailors ate the rats on board ships. What they didn't know was that they were protecting themselves against scurvy, because these furry little devils create their own vitamin C. In fact, most animals can make their own vitamin C in their bodies, but humans can't. Neither can monkeys, fruit bats, or, weirdly, guinea pigs. So, we have to get it from our food. We wouldn't recommend adding rat meat to your lunchbox, though.

on the move. Their rations were mostly coffee, pork, beans, and cornbread. So, scurvy thrived. And because the disease slowed the body's ability to heal itself, injured soldiers who came down with it were more likely to die from their wounds. Prisoners of war were also prone to scurvy due to harsh conditions and poor diet inside the prison camps.

Transporting citrus fruits from the tropical climates where they were grown to the battlefields where they were needed was a real challenge. Fortunately, people were starting to recognize that it wasn't just citrus that prevented scurvy, but all kinds of fruits and vegetables as well. Acting on this knowledge, Congress delivered its soldiers a new product called "desiccated vegetables." This was turnips, string beans, carrots, onions, and beets, all squished together and then dried into long bricks. But the men wouldn't always eat it, because it was gross. It probably didn't matter too much whether they ate their vegetable bricks or not, though. Because they had to be boiled for hours before they became edible, any nutrients the bricks contained were actually cooked out of them.

After a bad scurvy outbreak among Union troops in 1862, people began organizing food drives to supply soldiers with fresh vegetables. The main aim was to gather lots of potatoes and onions.

These were easily sourced and didn't spoil quickly and also seemed to ward off scurvy. People went from house to house collecting the veggies. They also held special events in which a potato or an onion was the entry fee. A sign was put up in Chicago that read, "Don't send your sweetheart a love-letter. Send him an onion." Such a romantic age.

For a long time, nobody knew why eating vegetables and fruit worked against scurvy. Why would sucking a sour lemon be any more effective than swigging sour sulfuric acid? It wasn't until the twentieth century that the pieces of the puzzle fell into place.

In 1928, a Hungarian scientist named Albert von Szent-Györgyi [Sent-Ghee-yur-ghee] discovered vitamin C, for which

ALBERT VON SZENT-GYÖRGYI

For a long time, nobody knew where the Inuit people—who live in the icy north where there's little vegetation—were getting their vitamin C. It turns out that because they eat raw meat and fish, they don't cook the vitamins out of their food. James Lind could have learned something from the Inuits. He wasted a lot of time trying to preserve the 'goodness" of lemons by cooking them and concentrating the juice. But the heating process often destroyed the vitamin C, which he didn't understand was the vital stuff that prevented scurvy.

Interestingly, guavas, bell peppers, and strawberries all contain more vitamin C than citrus fruits.

he won a Nobel Prize. Then, in 1933, a British guy named Sir Norman Haworth worked out the chemical structure of vitamin C. He showed that it helps us make collagen. Collagen is really important stuff that is found all over the body, in bones, muscles, tendons, and skin. It binds us together. Think of it like the cement that makes the bricks in a wall stick to one another. Without vitamin C, the "cement" inside us weakens, and we start to fall apart. That process of falling apart is what we call scurvy.

All those poorly supplied sailors and explorers in the past never stood a chance without farm-fresh produce in their bellies. So, we hope you learn from the mistakes of generations of sickly seafarers and listen to your folks when they tell you to eat your fruit and veggies!

Famous Deaths from Scurvy

1270: King Louis IX of France

Louis was a warrior king who took his army to fight in north Africa during the wars known as the Crusades. At first, he had a lot of victories, but his army eventually grew weak and sick. One writer at the time said that Louis's soldiers had painful problems with their gums—a sure sign of scurvy. Louis fell ill himself while laying siege to the city of Tunis. After he died, his body was carried back to his homeland. Along the route, crowds gathered to kneel as the dead king passed. Scientists later tested his jawbone and confirmed that Louis had scurvy at the time of his death.

1607: Bartholomew Gosnold, Explorer

Bartholomew was the captain of the *Godspeed*, one of three ships that sailed to the Americas in 1606. Even though he was the founder of Jamestown, the first permanent English settlement in the New World, and helped to design the fort for the Jamestown colony, he has been largely forgotten. A few months after he and his fellow colonizers landed in Virginia, he grew sick and died. It's a bit unclear, but scurvy may have helped finish him off. This was fourteen years before the more famous *Mayflower* pilgrims arrived in Massachusetts.

1736: Maria Pronchishcheva, Explorer

Maria was a Russian who sailed with her husband, Vasili, on a mission to map the shores of the Arctic Ocean. The voyage was successful, and they managed to chart a lot of coastline. On the return journey, as they camped at the mouth of a river, many of the crew fell ill with scurvy. Both Maria and Vasili died of the disease and were buried next to the river. A bay in the Laptev Sea is named after Maria—the first female polar explorer.

1741: Vitus Bering, Explorer

Though born in Denmark, Vitus did a lot of exploring for Peter the Great, the ruler of Russia. Vitus was the man who proved that North America and Asia aren't joined by land. His second big expedition was ordered by Empress Anna of Russia, and he spent nearly ten years mapping the northern coast of Russia, sailing as far as Alaska. He fell ill with scurvy on the return voyage and had to anchor at an island. He died there after a storm wrecked his ship. The Bering Strait is named after him.

1770: William Stark, Doctor and Early Dietician

William was an Englishman who experimented on himself in a series of twenty-four food trials to better understand the effects of different diets on the body. He first ate only bread and water for a month. Then he added other meaty and starchy foods. Within two months, his gums were swollen and bloody. By November 1769, he was living on nothing but honey pudding and cheese, though he allowed himself a few blackcurrants to celebrate Christmas. Just before he could begin the next phase, which would reintroduce fresh fruits and vegetables into his diet, he died from scurvy and malnutrition. But his detailed records of his experiments were useful to later scientists trying to figure out the importance of vitamin C.

AFTERWORD:
A "NOBEL" PURSUIT

T here you have it: you've made it safely to the end of our twisty-turny journey through the history of medicine. Along the way, we hope we've shown you that although humans have made a lot of progress and cured a lot of very bad diseases, doing so has often been a long and painful process. Figuring stuff out and changing minds sometimes takes centuries. But if you think that the kind of stubborn clinging to old ideas that you've read about here is a relic of the past, consider this . . .

For a long time, doctors were convinced that stomach ulcers were due to stress and poor diets, which caused some people to produce too much acid in their bellies. And this isn't ancient history, but a belief from around when your parents were born. Then, in the 1980s, an Australian doctor named Barry Marshall discovered that they are actually caused by a bacterium. But, just like poor Ignaz Semmelweis—who couldn't convince his work buddies to wash their hands in the nineteenth century—Barry had a lot of trouble making anyone listen to him. Doctors just wouldn't accept that their old ideas about ulcers were wrong. So, Barry decided to take matters into his own hands . . . literally.

One day, he picked up a petri dish full of the ulcer-causing bacteria and drank it. Soon afterward, he started having bad stomach cramps. Then came the puking and loss of appetite. At that point, Barry had some tests, which confirmed that he had indeed developed a stomach ulcer—just as he suspected he would. One course of antibiotics (thanks to our old friend, Alexander Fleming) and presto! Barry was right as rain.

In 2005, Barry and his research partner, Robin Warren, were given a Nobel Prize for their groundbreaking work.

Remember: sometimes, an idea takes hold and grows and everyone just accepts it. And sometimes it takes a really smart, determined, and brave person (or a whole long line of them) to question long-held beliefs. The world may not listen to these gutsy pioneers at first, but they're usually proved right in the end!

It's easy and fun to make jokes about strange medical ideas from history, which is why we do it quite a lot in this book. But it's important to remember that the doctors of the past, just like doctors today, were usually just trying to help people and were doing the best they could with the information and techniques that they had at the time. The world of science is always moving on. New medical discoveries are often built on ideas that have come before and add to the treasure chest of human knowledge.

So, when you look back and laugh at what people believed in the past, just ask yourself this: What will future generations think of us today?

ACKNOWLEDGMENTS

Writing a book is never easy, even in the best of circumstances. Adrian and I settled down to work on these pages just as a new virus was beginning to sweep across the world and shut down everyday life as we knew it. The general weirdness of writing a book about history's deadliest diseases during a global pandemic was not lost on us. Then, at the end of the process, I was diagnosed with early-stage breast cancer. The medical historian suddenly found herself in the role of patient.

Through all of this, we could not have squished and molded many centuries of medical stories into (we hope) a pleasing shape without the help of several people. First, we'd like to thank our editor, Megan Abbate, for helping us so brilliantly with the squishing and the molding. The title was a bit of a nightmare, but we got there in the end! Also, we'd like to thank our agent, Robert Guinsler, for his constant enthusiasm and guidance. And our manager, Jorge Hinojosa, who, for some reason, refuses to give up on us. A special thanks to Caroline Overy, whose careful reading of early drafts has made this a better book. And to John Candell, Bloomsbury's excellent designer, for helping to make this book look great.

Thanks, also, to our family, and our two fat cats, Oscar and Bobo, whose total lack of interest in the process of creating a book is oddly comforting.

SELECTED SOURCES

Lindsey has a PhD in the History of Science and Medicine and has studied the subject all her adult life. Here is a select number of sources that she has found useful over the years, and that helped in the making of this book. Adrian likes the ones with pictures in them.

Introduction

Fitzharris, Lindsey. *The Butchering Art: Joseph Lister's Quest to Transform the Grisly World of Victorian Medicine*. New York: Scientific American / Farrar, Straus and Giroux, 2017.

Fitzharris, Lindsey. "The Unsung Pioneer of Handwashing." *Wall Street Journal*, March 19, 2020.

Hollingham, Richard. *Blood and Guts: A History of Surgery*. London: BBC Books, 2008.

Nuland, Sherwin. *The Doctors' Plague: Germs, Childbed Fever, and the Strange Story of Ignác Semmelweis*. New York: W. W. Norton & Company, 2003.

Obenchain, *Theodore G. Genius Belabored: Childbed Fever and the Tragic Life of Ignaz Semmelweis*. Tuscaloosa: University of Alabama Press, 2016.

Porter, Roy. *Blood and Guts: A Short History of Medicine*. New York: W. W. Norton & Company, 2003.

Porter, Roy. *Disease, Medicine and Society in England, 1550–1860*. 2nd ed. Cambridge: Cambridge University Press, 1995.

Porter, Roy. *The Greatest Benefit to Mankind: A Medical History of Humanity*. New York: W. W. Norton & Company, 1998.

Semmelweis, Ignaz. *Etiology, Concept, and Prophylaxis of Childbed Fever* (1861). Translated by K. Kodell Carter. Madison: University of Wisconsin Press, 1983.

Sinclair, William. *Semmelweis: His Life and His Doctrine: A Chapter in the History of Medicine*. Manchester: University Press, 1909.

Youngson, A. J. *The Scientific Revolution in Victorian Medicine*. London: Croom Helm, 1979.

Plague

Benedictow, Ole J. *The Black Death 1346–1353: The Complete History*. Woodbridge: Boydell Press, 2006.

Blackmore, Erin. "Why Plague Doctors Wore Those Strange Beaked Masks." *National Geographic*, March 12, 2020.

Cantor, Norman F. *In the Wake of the Plague: The Black Death and the World it Made*. Rev. ed. New York: Simon & Schuster, 2015.

Green, Monica H. "The Four Black Deaths." *The American Historical Review* 125, no. 5 (December 2020): 1601–1631.

Green, Monica H. "How a Microbe Becomes a Pandemic: A New Story of the Black Death." *The Lancet Microbe* 1, no. 8 (December 2020): e311– e312.

Kohn, George C., ed. *Encyclopedia of Plague and Pestilence: From Ancient Times to the Present*. Rev. ed. New York: Checkmark Books, 2002.

Lawton, Graham. "How Many People Died Due to the Black Death in Europe?" *New Scientist*, May 25, 2022.

Mortimer, Ian. *The Time Traveller's Guide to Medieval England: A Handbook for Visitors to the Fourteenth Century*. New York: Touchstone Books, 2009.

Perry, David. "Did the Black Death Rampage across the World a Century Earlier Than Previously Thought?" *Smithsonian*, March 25, 2021.

Porter, Stephen. *Black Death: A New History of the Bubonic Plagues of London*. Stroud: Amberley Publishing, 2018.

Roberts, Ann. "The Plague in England." *History Today*, April 4, 1980.

Slack, Paul. *Plague: A Very Short Introduction*. Oxford: Oxford University Press, 2012.

Smallpox

Bazin, Hervé. *The Eradication of Smallpox: Edward Jenner and the First and Only Eradication of a Human Infectious Disease.* San Diego: Academic Press, 2000.

Bennett, Michael. "Jenner's Ladies: Women and Vaccination against Smallpox in Early Nineteenth-Century Britain." *History* 93, no. 4 (October 2008): 497–513.

Brunton, Deborah. *The Politics of Vaccination: Practice and Policy in England, Wales, Ireland, and Scotland, 1800–1874.* Rochester: University of Rochester Press, 2008.

Fisher, Richard B. *Edward Jenner, 1749–1823.* London: André Deutsch Limited, 1991.

Hopkins, Donald R. *The Greatest Killer: Smallpox in History.* Rev. ed. Chicago: The University of Chicago Press, 2002.

Jewson, N. D. "Medical Knowledge and the Patronage System in 8th Century England." *Sociology* 8, no. 3 (September 1974): 369–385.

Miller, Genevieve. *The Adoption of Inoculation for Smallpox in England and France.* Philadelphia: University of Pennsylvania Press, 2018.

Porter, Dorothy, and Roy Porter. *Patient's Progress: Doctors and Doctoring in Eighteenth-Century England.* Cambridge: Polity Press, 1989.

Rusnock, Andrea. "Catching Cowpox: The Early Spread of Smallpox Vaccination, 1798–1810." *Bulletin of the History of Medicine* 83, no. 1 (Spring 2009): 17–36.

Williamson, Stanley. *The Vaccination Controversy: The Rise, Reign and Fall of Compulsory Vaccination for Smallpox.* Liverpool: Liverpool University Press, 2007.

Rabies

Debré, Patrice. *Louis Pasteur.* Translated by Elborg Forster. Baltimore: Johns Hopkins University Press, 1998.

Dubos, René. *Pasteur and Modern Science.* Thomas D. Brock, ed. Washington, DC: ASM Press, 1998.

Nicolle, Jacques. *Louis Pasteur. A Master of Scientific Enquiry.* London: The Scientific Book Guild, 1962.

Pearce, J. "Louis Pasteur and Rabies: A Brief Note." *Journal of Neurology, Neurosurgery & Psychiatry* 73 (2002): 82.

Pemberton, Neil, and Michael Worboys. *Mad Dogs and Englishmen: Rabies in Britain, 1830–2000.* London: Palgrave Macmillan, 2007.

Teal, Adrian. *The Gin Lane Gazette: A Profusely Illustrated Compendium of Devilish Scandal & Oddities from the Darkest Recesses of Georgian England.* ·London: Unbound, 2012.

Théodoridès, J. "Pasteur and Rabies: The British Connection." *Journal of the Royal Society of Medicine* 82, no. 8 (August 1989): 488–490.

Vallery-Radot, René. *The Life of Pasteur.* Translated by R. L. Devonshire. Westminster: Archibald Constable & Co., 1902.

Walton, John K. "Mad Dogs and Englishmen: The Conflict over Rabies in Late Victorian England." *Journal of Social History* 13, no. 2 (Winter 1979): 219–239.

Wasik, Bill, and Monica Murphy. *Rabid: A Cultural History of the World's Most Diabolical Virus.* New York: Viking, 2012.

Worboys, Michael. "Mad Cows, French Foxes and Other Rabid Animals in Britain, 1800 to the Present." *Veterinary History* 18, no. 4 (February 2017): 543–567.

Tuberculosis

Barberis, I., N. L. Bragazzi, L. Galluzzo, and M. Martini. "The History of Tuberculosis: From the First Historical Records to the Isolation of Koch's Bacillus." *Journal of Preventive Medicine and Hygiene* 58, no. 1 (March 2017): E9–E12.

Brock, Thomas D. *Robert Koch: A Life in Medicine and Bacteriology.* Berlin: Springer, 1988.

Bynum, Helen. *Spitting Blood: The History of Tuberculosis*. Oxford: Oxford University Press, 2012.

Clavin, Tom. *Dodge City: Wyatt Earp, Bat Masterson, and the Wickedest Town in the American West*. New York: St. Martin's Press, 2017.

Daniel, Thomas M. *Captain of Death: The Story of Tuberculosis*. Rochester: University of Rochester Press, 1998.

Gradmann, Christoph. *Laboratory Disease: Robert Koch's Medical Bacteriology*. Translated by Elborg Forster. Baltimore: Johns Hopkins University Press, 2009.

Lougheed, Kathryn. *Catching Breath: The Making and Unmaking of Tuberculosis*. London: Bloomsbury Sigma, 2017.

Luca, Simona, and Traian Mihaescu. "History of BCG Vaccine." *Maedica* 8, no. 1 (March 2013): 53–58.

Murphy, Jim, and Alison Blank. *Invincible Microbe: Tuberculosis and the Never-Ending Search for a Cure*. New York: Clarion Books, 2012.

Murray, John F., Dean E. Schraufnagel, and Philip C. Hopewell. "Treatment of Tuberculosis. A Historical Perspective." *Annals of the American Thoracic Society* 12, no. 12 (December 2015): 1749–1759.

Roberts, Gary L. *Doc Holliday: The Life and Legend*. Hoboken: Wiley, 2006.

Cholera

Ackerknecht, Erwin H. "Anticontagionism between 1821 and 1867." *Bulletin of the History of Medicine* 22 (1948): 562–593.

Cicak, Tessa, and Nicola Tynan. "Mapping London's Water Companies and Cholera Deaths." *The London Journal* 40, no. 1 (March 2015): 21–32.

Durey, Michael. *The Return of the Plague: British Society and the Cholera 1831–2*. Dublin: Gill and Macmillan, 1979.

Fitzharris, Lindsey. *The Butchering Art: Joseph Lister's Quest to Transform the Grisly World of Victorian Medicine*. New York: Scientific American / Farrar, Straus and Giroux, 2017.

Gaw, Jerry L. *"A Time to Heal": The Diffusion of Listerism in Victorian Britain.* Philadelphia: American Philosophical Society, 1999.

Hardy, Anne. "Water and the Search for Public Health in London in the Eighteenth and Nineteenth Centuries." *Medical History* 28, no. 3 (July 1984): 250–282.

Johnson, Steven. *The Ghost Map: A Street, an Epidemic and the Hidden Power of Urban Networks.* New York: Riverhead Books, 2006.

Morris, R. J. *Cholera, 1832: The Social Response to an Epidemic.* New York: Holmes & Meier,1976.

Pelling, Margaret. *Cholera, Fever, and English Medicine, 1825–1865.* Oxford: Oxford University Press, 1978.

Pelling, Margaret. "Epidemics in Nineteenth-Century British Towns: How Important Was Cholera?" *Journal of Victorian Culture* 27, no. 2 (2022): 346–355.

Rosenberg, Charles E. *Explaining Epidemics and Other Studies in the History of Medicine.* Cambridge: Cambridge University Press, 1992.

Snow, John. *Snow on Cholera: Being a Reprint of Two Papers.* Wade H. Frost, ed. New York and London: Hafner Publishing, 1965.

Taylor-Pirie, Emily. *Empire Under the Microscope: Parasitology and the British Literary Imagination, 1885–1935.* London: Palgrave Macmillan, 2021.

Thomas, Amanda J. *Cholera: The Victorian Plague.* Bransley: Pen and Sword History, 2015.

Worboys, Michael. *Spreading Germs: Disease Theories and Medical Practice in Britain, 1865–1900.* Cambridge: Cambridge University Press, 2000.

Scurvy

Baron, Jeremy Hugh. "Sailors' Scurvy before and after James Lind—a Reassessment." *Nutrition Reviews* 67, no. 6 (June 2009): 315–332.

Brown, Stephen R. *Scurvy: How a Surgeon, a Mariner and a Gentleman Solved the Greatest Medical Mystery of the Age of Sail.* New York: Thomas Dunne Books, 2004.

Carpenter, Kenneth J. *The History of Scurvy and Vitamin C*. Cambridge: Cambridge University Press, 1986.

Cook, Gordon C. "Scurvy in the British Mercantile Marine in the 19th Century, and the Contribution of the Seamen's Hospital Society." *Postgraduate Medical Journal* 80, no. 942 (2004): 224–229.

Harrison, Mark. "Scurvy on Sea and Land: Political Economy and Natural History, c. 1780–c.1850." *Journal for Maritime Research* 15, no. 1 (May 2013): 7–15.

Harvie, David I. *Limeys: The Conquest of Scurvy*. Stroud: Sutton Publishing Limited, 2002.

Lamb, Jonathan. *Scurvy: The Disease of Discovery*. Princeton: Princeton University Press, 2016.

Walter, Richard. *Anson's Voyage round the World in the Years 1740–44*. Percy G. Adams, ed. New York: Dover Publications Inc., 1974.

Afterword

Abbott, A. "Medical Nobel Awarded for Ulcers." *Nature*, October 3, 2005.

Charities, Hanno. "When Scientists Experiment on Themselves: H. pylori and Ulcers." *Scientific American*, July 5, 2014.

Weintraub, Pamela. "The Doctor Who Drank Infectious Broth, Gave Himself an Ulcer, and Solved a Medical Mystery." *Discover*, April 8, 2010.

FURTHER READING FOR FUTURE
MEDICAL HISTORIANS

Hudson, Briony. *Medicine: A Magnificently Illustrated History*. London: Big Picture Press, 2022.

Ignotofsky, Rachel. *Women in Science: 50 Fearless Pioneers Who Changed the World*. Berkeley: Ten Speed Press, 2016.

Jenner, Greg. *You Are History: From the Alarm Clock to the Toilet, the Amazing History of the Things You Use Every Day*. London: Walker Books, 2022.

Kang, Lydia, and Nate Pedersen. *Patient Zero: A Curious History of the World's Worst Diseases*. New York: Workman Publishing Company, 2021.

Kang, Lydia, and Nate Pedersen. *Quackery: A Brief History of the Worst Ways to Cure Everything*. New York: Workman Publishing Company, 2017.

Kay, Adam. *Kay's Anatomy: A Complete (and Completely Disgusting) Guide to the Human Body*. London: Puffin, 2020.

Kay, Adam. *Kay's Marvellous Medicine: A Gross and Gruesome History of the Human Body*. London: Puffin, 2021.

Morris, Thomas. *The Mystery of Exploding Teeth and Other Curiosities from the History of Medicine*. London: Dutton, 2018.

Mould, Steve. *The Bacteria Book: Gross Germs, Vile Viruses, and Funky Fungi*. London: DK Children, 2018.

Paxton, Jennifer Z., and Katy Wiedemann. *Anatomicum*. London: Big Picture Press, 2019.

Payne, Kev. *Gross and Ghastly: Human Body: The Big Book of Disgusting Human Body Facts*. London: DK Children, 2021.

Tiner, John. *Exploring the History of Medicine: From the Ancient Physicians of Pharaoh to Genetic Engineering*. Eastbourne: New Leaf Publishing, 1999.

Washington, Danni. *Bold Women in Science: 15 Women in History You Should Know*. New York: Rockridge Press, 2021.

INDEX